FOREVER IN YOUR DEBT

A Christian's Guide To Health, Happiness and Contentment

Dr. Nick Dreliozis, DC

I&L Publishing

COPYRIGHT ©2003

**Forever
In Your Debt**

by

Dr. Nick Dreliozis, DC

ALL RIGHTS RESERVED. NO PART OF THIS BOOK MAY BE REPRODUCED IN ANY FORM OR BY ANY ELECTRONIC OR MECHANICAL MEANS INCLUDING INFORMATION STORAGE AND RETRIEVAL SYSTEMS WITHOUT THE PERMISSION IN WRITING FROM THE AUTHOR OR PUBLISHER EXCEPT FOR A REVIEWER WHO MAY QUOTE BRIEF PASSAGES IN A REVIEW.

ISBN 1-930002-50-5

I & L PUBLISHING
174 OAK DR. PKWY.
OROVILLE, CA 95966
PH: (530) 589-5048
FX: (530) 589-3551

FIRST EDITION

**FOR ORDERING AND DISTRIBUTING CONTACT
I & L PUBLISHING**

Printed in the United States by Morris Publishing
3212 East Highway 30
Kearney, NE 68847
1-800-650-7888

Table of Contents

To The Reader

Chapter 1:	Incorporate Religion Into Your Life	1
Chapter 2:	A Simple Review Of The Bible	17
Chapter 3:	What Does It Mean To Be A Christian?	49
Chapter4:	The Compass	67
Chapter 5:	The Golden Rule	78
Chapter 6:	The Treadmill	92
Chapter 7:	To Be Or Not To Be…A Copycat	100
Chapter 8:	Do Not Be A Slave	110
Chapter 9:	Get Ready	125
Chapter 10:	Forever In Your Debt	157

Front Cover

The beautiful stream shown on the front cover is the Alphio River, pronounced "Al-Fee-Oh". It is located near the village of Matesi, in Greece, and was not very far from Nick Dreliozis' birthplace.

Some of Nick's inspiration to write this book came while walking along the rocky shoreline of this fast-moving stream.

The ideas and desire to have a life of peace and harmony in the midst of the raging current of life is partly due to the time spent at the Alphio River.

To The Reader

I sincerely hope you will enjoy this book!

I have spent many years developing an easy and systematic way of finding health, happiness and contentment. I know you can find it also; and this book will help you.

The first time reading this book, read at a regular pace.

Then read at a slower pace the second time around.

The more times you read it, the more you will get out of it.

We as Christians need all the help we can get. The Devil wants to rob us from ever finding a healthy, happy and content lifestyle. Our Great Lord certainly wants us to be healthy, happy and content forever.

Please tell your friends about this book, and always keep your hope alive with good things to come your way.

Nick Dreliozis

Chapter One

INCORPORATE RELIGION INTO YOUR LIFE

The first and most important thing of all is to immediately incorporate religion into your life. I realize that you might have heard this a thousand and one times from a minister, friend, or some television Evangelist. But to do this is not as easy as it might sound. We often hear, "Go to Church and everything will be alright." This has always reminded me of when people would say, "Now be a good boy or be a good girl." It is likely that, in your entire life, you never had anyone explain how to implement a simple, systematic way of incorporating religion into your life. Most of our parents simply tell us to go to Church, and ministers confirm this.

I believe that just going to Church or attending Church is not religion. We must have a reason to go; and when we attend, what are we supposed to get out of it? We are bombarded with all kinds of information from magazines and television that we read and view on a daily basis.

They tell us how we can become happy, healthy and rich, after awhile we believe all of this mumbo-jumbo and are caught up by man's view of what is important.

We must personally develop a systematic way of incorporating religion into our lives. Otherwise, we will be swallowed up by other people's view on what health, happiness, and contentment are all about rather than our good Lord's intentions for us.

The best place to start in trying to figure out the secrets to a healthier life, a happier life, and a more content life is to go to the beginning of it all. The beginning for us Christians is to understand the advice and teachings of the Bible. Most families have a Bible; but more often than not it collects dust in some drawer or on a shelf. Even as a young boy and as a young adult, I didn't know anything about the Bible. Even though I grew up in a Christian family and went to Church all the time, I just felt as though I was going through the motions. Later on in my life I found out from other members my age and older, that almost everyone just went through the motions. They were in the same boat as I was. We went to Church because our parents did, which is fine as a young person, but it was merely a habit. We were never taught how to use religion in a practical way that would help our day-to-day-lives.

Forever in Your Debt

As a 12-year-old, I remember one of the rewards that were given to all of us Sunday School children. It was a Bible with our name engraved on the outside covers. I appreciated mine. I thought it was pretty special that someone took the time and effort to engrave my name on it. However like all of the other children, I put it in a drawer where it stayed for many years. After all, I remember thinking that the Bible must be like those schoolbooks I had read at school. The last thing on my mind was to read another book, especially that Bible book. I opened it once just to look at the cool pictures inside. But looking at the words totally turned me off. It was easy to turn me off since I couldn't even understand it! To the very best of my ability, the only words I could understand were words like "the" or the letter "a". Everything else seemed to be in another language.

That Bible book did lie in that drawer for many years and it never crossed my mind to pick it up again.

Just like everyone else, the years went by and High School graduation came and went. At that point in my life, I knew I wanted to go to college and most important of all, I wanted to find out the meaning of life and had a further desire to find God's purpose for my life. I was eighteen years old at the time, and this burning desire to find Spiritual answers was within me.

At the end of the first semester of college, there was a terrible snowstorm. Some of you in the MidWest might recall the Winter storm of 1978. It was a terrible snowstorm. Virtually every business and school was closed due to the bad weather. I was home from college, and was bored out of my mind. Everyone was cooped up with nothing to do. After eating everything in sight and after watching way too much television, I became desperate. In looking for things to do, I opened the drawer that my old Bible was in. It was in the same spot that I had left it years ago. Though it was dusty, it was in excellent shape. I was a little surprised to see it in such good shape, but I shouldn't have been; after all, things usually don't wear out unless you use them! I began to read it like a person would read any book. My Bible was the King James Version. I still use the King James Version to this day but at that time it was even more difficult to understand. I did not accomplish much that first evening of reading the Bible. In fact, as I vaguely recall, I fell asleep shortly after beginning to read it.

I was determined to keep trying to read it. Every few nights I would pick it up and start reading it as if it was any other book. I think I just wanted to finish it. As I was reading it I felt as though there was something contained in that book that was important. Even though I tried to read it for a long while, I was getting frustrated in that it didn't make a lot of sense to me and it was extremely boring. Inevitably, whenever I read it in the evening, before going to bed, it always had the same three-fold affect on me: I knew it was important, it confused me, and it was an excellent natural sedative!

The fact that I couldn't understand it didn't bother me as much as my inability to apply it to my day-to-day life. I reasoned that this had to be due to the writers of the Bible not writing well; perhaps they even intentionally made it difficult to understand! What a bright first year college student I must have been! After being frustrated with not understanding the Bible, I placed it back in the home it had come to know for all of those years. Yes, it went back into that drawer to collect more dust.

Even though I felt that I didn't get anything out of reading the Bible, I knew that I needed to pray daily. I remember praying throughout the remainder of my college days. I can't remember what I prayed for or what I said. I guess it didn't matter how I said something or what I said. It seemed to me that the most important thing was that I was praying to a Superior Being.

Besides praying, I would often ask other people what they thought of the Bible and religion in general. Some people had an opinion on this topic and others couldn't care less. There were many differing opinions. The greater the variety of opinions I encountered, the more determined I was to find answers on religion, health, happiness and contentment.

Though I didn't fully realize it at the time, I had a burning desire to find the truth about religion and the secrets to having a happier life. This was very important to me. I knew that if I lived a long time, this information would certainly help me with the quality of my life. I am not certain why, or even how I began to think this way.

The views on religion that I would hear from my friends sounded convincing. However, when I would observe their lives something did not fit. What they were saying and how they lived were at odds with one another. I noticed something peculiar about a certain group of people who would go to Church, quote the Bible verbatim, and speak of Jesus as though they have met Him personally. However, these same people would scream at their children, marry and then divorce at the first sign of difficulty and party like there was no tomorrow. Most of these Bible-beaters did not appear happy at all. Trouble seemed to follow them wherever they went. This is not something that I observed in college life but this was a general observation out in the community. To make matters even more personal, I also knew two Pastors who talked of religion in a hearty way but sure didn't live it. In trying to piece things together throughout all of this turmoil, I had no answers of my own but I knew the things that I was observing did not appear right.

Deep down inside, I continued to look for answers to a happy, healthier, more content, and less stressful way of life. The search continued throughout my college days. Closing in on my final days in college I had not found the right answers though I had diligently tried to piece things together. Time was running out. I was beginning to think that I would never find the answers I was looking for. It shows you how despondent I was at the time. In a last ditch effort I approached an individual whom I admired very much. This particular person was in his fifties while I was a young man in my early twenties. This gentleman was like a mentor to me. Through the years, I had somehow never asked this man his views on basic life questions such as health, happiness, and contentment. Maybe I was just too close to him or maybe I didn't want to appear ignorant to him. After all, a nearly graduated college student should have the basics of life down pat. Right?

Dr. Nick Dreliozis

This gentleman was a successful businessman, married with two children and went to Church on Sundays. What a perfect person to ask! I knew that if I went to him, he would share with me all of his wisdom and give me practical advice on how to be content, happy and healthy.

I approached him and asked him my burning questions. He told me that I should go to Church to find the answers. Though he may not have been aware of it, I had been going to Church sporadically. However, after my conversation with him, I thought to myself that I might be going to the wrong Church. I thought perhaps I should attend his. After all, he was a lot older than I was, as well as more successful; and everything seemed to be going his way. At last, I attended his Church. Once I had made this decision, something inside me told me to talk to another person that was a friend of my mentor. I just felt that I might garner even more wisdom as I encountered others who were acquainted with my mentor. I really felt silly and stupid asking someone else about my mentor. I was certain they thought I must be off my rocker to question certain aspects of this man.

The "wake up call" came when I asked a particular acquaintance his views of my mentor. I was shocked to discover that the image I'd had of my mentor was not an accurate picture at all.

Forever in Your Debt

People that intimately knew my mentor were painting a picture of him that was foreign to me. How could I be so wrong in seeing this man as being so perfect? Could it have been that my burning desire to find someone with their act together clouded my vision? Could it all have been simply a "good act" by my mentor friend, or could it have been that I was not as smart as I'd thought?

I found out from several sources that he was on his third wife, was always working and was never home. He had children with his previous wives and yet never took time to see them nor supported them. He had jumped from Church to Church and would never settle down. Also, that wonderful business that he had with lots of customers was heavily in debt and was ready to go under.

Not too long after these events, his business did go bankrupt. He got another divorce, changed Churches and I am sure the story continues. All of this was devastating to me. At the time I was discovering this information, I simply did not want to believe it. I was wishing that I'd never asked questions in the first place. Finding the truth sometimes can really hurt. You might know what I am talking about. How could it be? My mentor that had appeared so successful, so happy, so healthy, so content and so religious was not that way at all. At that point in my life, I felt hopeless in finding the answers I so desperately needed.

I finally graduated and moved to the town where I grew up. Even though I felt that I received a good education, I still was not fulfilled in my Spiritual life. Once back home and puttering around the house I'd grown up in, I went to the drawer where I'd left my personalized Bible. I can't remember exactly what led me to open that drawer again, but something did. Over the years I've found that this "inner voice" which speaks to me quite often leads me to something good. Not to my surprise, once again, the Bible had a layer of dust on it and had not moved at all since the last time I had picked it up. It had been many years since I'd first received it. It now looked like a very old Bible. Then an amazing thing happened. As I wiped off the dust, the Bible appeared to become new again! Even as a college graduate who thought he knew everything, I should have been able to reason that if I hadn't used the Bible, it would not wear out.

This time I was determined to pick up this Bible book and give an honest effort to learn something worth learning. When I made this commitment I realized that all the previous years I had been putting faith in fallible *people*. I was also looking for life's greatest mysteries through *people*. I was putting way too much stock in *people*. This time I was going to allow the scriptures of the Bible to guide me. No longer was I going to put my faith in any person, place or thing.

That Bible that I picked up then is the same one that I use now. Fortunately, in the back, it had a summary and guide. I used to think that the Bible was just a book written by one particular person. However, that little summary at the back made me realize the Bible was a collection of writings that were written by several different people throughout time. I also quickly realized that these people were inspired and directed by God Himself to give us a roadmap to follow during our brief lives. More and more, these things began to make sense.

As I was beginning to ever so slowly piece it together, I could only think of two things. One was that even though I had completed college and learned a lot, I had not even scratched the surface about learning things that were really important. Secondly, I could have kicked myself for spending all that time and energy trying to find out the secrets about life, religion, health, happiness and contentment through *people* rather than God Himself! The only thing I got out of it was empty answers and more confusion. After getting over the frustration of wasting my time in college, I now know that people do not have the answers to everything. However, the Good Lord had the answers back then...and He still does today?

This leather bound book with my name engraved on it was not just a book after all. This Bible book had advice and answers in it. These answers and advice were written during widely differing times throughout history. All of these writings were from around 1500 BC to 100 AD. The more I read that summary portion in the back, the more I could understand. Though I still had not "put it all together" at this point, it was a beginning for me. I continued to be assured that I was getting God's point of view on things rather than relying on man's point of view. I knew that these writings could bring me good instead of bad, happiness instead of sorrow, and contentment instead of despair. Most important of all, I knew that these writings would give me hope for the future and hope in God instead of hopelessness in everything.

The answers to the questions I had been searching for were slowly beginning to come and a sense of joy was coming upon me. In learning more about the Bible, I found that not only there were different writings in the Bible but all of those writings or books were divided into two different sections. One section was referred to as the Old Testament and the other section was the New Testament. The Old Testament contained 39 books (or writings), and the New Testament contained 27 books (or writings). I continued to believe that if I could find some way to understand how this Bible book was put together, and why it was written, then I could find the answers to the secrets of health, happiness, contentment and harmony.

The Bible, as I found out, was not only divided into two sections but was written by different people. Some of these people who wrote these books are known and some are not known. The unknown people would be similar to unknown authors we hear about from time to time. It didn't seem to matter to me who the authors were. It could have been written by a male, or a female, a peasant or a King; it simply did not matter who wrote it. What mattered was for me to learn and understand the material contained in it.

I needed to understand this material at least to the degree that I could use it for the remainder of my life. Even though it is never too late to learn, I felt that the sooner I could learn the important issues about life, the better off I would be.
As I think about it, how can a person travel through life if they don't have the tools of knowledge to help them find a happier, healthier, and more contented life? If a person were to rely on trial and error, it would take them a whole lifetime to figure things out. Who would want to waste their whole life in

trial and error only to come to this conclusion? Certainly not me. I wanted those tools of knowledge to use…right away!

The more I learned, the better I felt about everything. One of the simple things I learned that really impacted me was finding out what the word *testament* meant. This word *testament* means agreement. It was a word that represented an agreement with the Israelites and God himself. For whatever reason, God chose the Israelites to contract this agreement with. It was an agreement based on honor and trust. God would take care of His people, the Israelites. He would take care of their Spiritual needs, their physical needs and anything else that life would bring upon them. The only thing God wanted of them was for them to obey His voice, commune with Him and only have one God that they trusted in. This God was invisible. They could not see Him, but by faith they knew He was there.

In my mind, I reason that God is like air. Everyone knows that it is there and without it we will die. We cannot see the air, but it keeps filling our lungs so we can survive. We don't think about the air in every breath that we take but we know it will be there and don't worry about it. The Israelites were in the same kind of situation. God told them that He was there and would continue to be there for them. The only thing that they would have to do is trust in Him, follow His laws and pray for help and guidance.

All 39 books of the Old Testament were written before Jesus was sent down to us. These books were written by a wide variety of people but they were all instructed by God on what to write. These books contain the history of how we were created, some history on religion, how to praise God, and the Israelite's struggles. The last, and most important thing contained in these writings was the promise that one day there would be this great Savior to come and deliver the Israelites.

This Great Savior of the Israelites eventually would be the Savior of all mankind. He would show a way for anyone in the World that would listen. Also, He was not merely and Earthly Savior. He was not going to merely save them from the evil people of their times, but would save them from *themselves* and their sins. This Great Savior, which had the power then and has the power now to bring us health, happiness, harmony, and contentment is JESUS CHRIST.

Leaders of their respective Synagogues read these Old Testament books to the Jewish people. This was so they would not forget whom they were and whom they were to wait for. Then, finally the time had come for God to reveal Himself in bodily form to the human race. This had been prophesied hundreds of years earlier by the Prophet Daniel. However, as unbelievable as it may seem, God's chosen people (the Israelites) rejected Him as being their promised Messiah. They arranged for Him to be crucified so they could keep their "Religious System" intact. But this was all part of His master plan. God then decided to allow "whosoever" to be God's chosen people. This included both Jews (the predominant Israeli Tribe) and Gentiles (non-Jews) to be God's chosen people.

The 27 New Testament books told this story. It revealed God's new agreement with all mankind, no matter what nationality they were. The Great Master Architect of this new agreement is Jesus Christ our Savior. Whosoever will believe upon Him as being the long promised Messiah will become one of God's chosen people!

Chapter Two

A SIMPLE REVIEW OF THE Bible

I would like to share with you a little story about my mother. When I was child, my mother would keep active and busy. She cooked for our family like a good mother should. In the kitchen, she prepared basic good and nutritious foods. She did not have time to be creative in the kitchen nor did she want to be creative. She always thought she had other things that needed to get done and creative cooking was not one of them! As she got older and all of us children were out of the house, she got a part-time job at a local coffee/sandwich shop. She really enjoyed it and the owner wanted to increase the items that they served. The owner wanted to add "Quiche" to the menu.

For some reason my mother didn't want to attempt this. Perhaps this is because she was always used to making basic foods. The sandwich shop owner happened to be a very nice lady. She assured my mother that Quiche was not difficult to make. I remember my mother not only calling me, but my sisters too. She was dreading that her boss was going to have her make this new item that she couldn't even pronounce! For whatever reason, my mother had it in her head that she could never learn to make Quiche. Thus, she did not even want to try.

After much discussion, the coffee shop owner finally convinced my mother to at least observe her preparing Quiche. She reluctantly watched and to her surprise, this "foreign sounding thing" was not very difficult for her to make after all! She learned how to make it well. She enjoyed making it so much that every time we would come home to visit, there was Quiche waiting. A very difficult thing to learn in my mother's mind was now "a snap"!

Understanding the Bible is sort of like this also. Sometimes a person doesn't know where to start. But once a person starts to understand the Bible, they want to learn from it more often. The New Testament of the Bible has 27 books in it. Just like the Old Testament, men also wrote it. God wanted these men to write down certain words or messages so His words could remain forever in print for the World to benefit from. This was not a business for God. He would get no royalties. However, it would erase the possibility of mankind claiming ignorance as an excuse for not knowing about God. Everyone in the World would have a "roadmap" that they could reference as they traveled along life's pathway.

This New Testament is very different from the Old Testament. This time the new agreement would be with anyone that would listen, for generations to come. Jesus came down from Heaven to be Earth born in Bethlehem as a Jew. He came to show us a new way. God wanted everyone to continue to obey God's law. However, He wanted to add to it for the betterment for all of His people.

As a man, His mission was to prove to everyone that there was an Almighty God up above. He also wanted us to be warned that there was a powerful bad Spirit that also existed. This bad Spirit was the Devil. This Devil wants us to be miserable, less happier, more stressed out, less content and totally unhealthy.

Jesus came to give us the "wake up call" and also to give us the tools to fight against this ever-present bad Spirit. He said that the Devil could be neutralized and defeated. This could be done by praying, focusing on God's words that are written in the Bible, and believing that there is a good Lord up above that can do anything.

This Son of God's name is Jesus (which means Savior). He inevitably had to show the World that he was the Son of God. He had to perform the greatest miracle in the history of mankind. To witness the greatest miracle ever performed He chose twelve men of His time. These men were going to see what Jesus could do and tell the World of the great power of this man filled with God's Spirit. These twelve men were later referred to as Jesus' Apostles. Jesus told these men that He would be put to death. And then, after He was dead for three days He would rise again by the power of God.

    This greatest miracle of all would be to give everyone in the World Hope. An even greater miracle would be for the Hope to follow for generations! Whether we are male or female; whether we are young or old; whether we are white, brown or black, there is hope for us all. We can all get to a place called Paradise. This place called Paradise is for everyone. It is a place where we can be forever not only a few years, but for millions of years...for eternity! In order to be ushered into Paradise we must believe what Jesus stood for. Along with believing what he stood for, we must also follow through with some other things. We have to stop abusing ourselves with the bad things we do as people. Also we have to treat other people like we would like to be treated.

    This sounds simple enough to do but "follow through" can be very difficult. It is similar to physical exercise. We all know that exercise is good for us and not too difficult to do once we begin, but for some reason the majority of people do not do it.

Jesus said that everyone can get into the Kingdom of Heaven. And, it is never too late to make the decision to get into Paradise. The good LORD wants us all to be with Him. The Devil wants to fill your heart and mine with the seeds of sadness. The Devil wants us to abuse ourselves. The Devil wants to put strife, unkindness and hatred between us and our families and friends. He wants you and me to fail the task and not get into paradise.

I believe we should prepare to live forever in Paradise. We prepare for everything else in our lives. We prepare to go to work. We prepare for a vacation that we might want to take. We almost always prepare for dinner. Lord knows we can't do without that. Doesn't it make sense to prepare to get into Paradise?

Jesus, the only Son of God, came down to show us the way of life by sacrificing Himself. However, He began his life in a quiet way. He was born in a place that we would call a barn today. His Earthly parents were in a neighboring town that was quite a distance from home. In trying to find a place to stay, they found nothing available. They went to different Inns to find a place, but the only thing they found was an unfriendly voice at each door saying that they were full. We sometimes feel that the times we live in are more corrupt and evil than those of many years ago. However, during Jesus' time, people were just as bad and cold-hearted. These cold-hearted Innkeepers saw this woman was pregnant and yet refused to find a spot for her. Their cold hearts did not realize that the child that she was carrying would one day be able to save their miserable lives. If only they had known....

Mary and Joseph were rejected again and again in their search for a place to rest for the night. Finally, the place they found was in a barn. This barn was where God's child would be born. There would be no Media hype, no fanfare and certainly no modern conveniences.

On a cold, dark, December night with no doctor or midwife, a baby was born that would change the World in a better way. This baby was like any other baby at the beginning. He came out crying, needing His mother. A plain and simple beginning was destined for this baby.

Most of us with children know in advance what our child is to be named. We thought about it many times before our child was born. Sometimes we choose names that we just simply like. Other times we choose a name in remembrance of a loved one. In Joseph's and the Virgin Mary's case, the name was already chosen for them. They did not really have to think about it at all.

God knew to send an Angel to Mary to inform her of His plans before she was to supernaturally conceive the Christ child. Needless to say, for Mary to become pregnant and claim that she had no sexual relations with anyone would be absolutely unbelievable. And, even more than today, it was totally unacceptable to become pregnant prior to marriage. Gabriel, the Messenger from God, comforted her by saying that she was not alone and God was with her. He went on to also say that God had chosen her to carry this baby in her womb. The Angel explained that she should not be afraid. Instead she should be glad! This child would be the one that had been Prophesied about hundreds of years before. The baby that she was carrying in her womb was going to change mankind forever. Her response to this news was simply, "I am the Lord's Servant. May it be to me as you have said." Then the Angel left her.

Shortly thereafter, Joseph was considering ending his relationship with his Fiancée, Mary. However, an Angel of God appeared to Joseph in a dream. He told him that his future wife was clean from any wrongdoing. The Angel instructed Joseph that he should continue on with his plans to marry her. You see, in those days a man would be required to marry a woman only if he had gotten her pregnant.

The Angel had instructed Mary that the name of her newborn baby was to be Jesus. In Hebrew, the name Jesus means Savior. It was not Mary's decision to use this name. It was God's. When the baby was born, she followed the Angel's instructions naming the infant, Jesus. She knew that God's Spirit was in this young child.

I recall reading this story in my BIBLE for the first time. To imagine that these events actually took place two thousand years ago was mind-boggling! I began to think that I was finally finding the secret of health, happiness and contentment. Even though it was not in "black and white", I knew I was onto something! It was like some kind of good Spirit coming into me and beginning to make me feel better and somehow telling me what to do. It was as if a sense of right and wrong was being revealed to me without any words spoken, but mostly a feeling. Since I was feeling better about the direction I was going, I continued to read my Bible. I was trying not to just memorize things, but to understand things. My goal in reading the BIBLE was to "get to the point" rather than to just memorize the words or verses.

The Biblical account of Jesus being born in a barn with only His Earthly father and mother present did not pick up again until this child was twelve years old. The events take place in the outdoor market square; perhaps the middle of town. Jesus and his parents were in Jerusalem for the Feast of the Passover, according to Jewish Custom. He somehow got separated from his parents as He was drawn like a magnet to a place they called a Synagogue. This was where the Jewish people would go and worship God. It was also the place where the elders of the Church would read passages of the Old Testament to the Congregation

This was done for many reasons. The Jewish people had a long, hard history. They wanted to praise God for taking them out of bondage from Egypt. They did not want to forget about God's promise to be their God. They wanted their children to always remember their peculiar ways and most important of all, they wanted to remember that God had promised them that He was going to send a Messiah to them. This Messiah would set them forever free from their enemies.

This twelve-year-old boy, Jesus, had drifted from his parents to the Synagogue and had participated in the service that day. And He astonished every person in that Holy Temple. He not only was an observer of the Service, but went up to the pulpit and started to read the Old Testament writings without anyone asking him. This kind of act was unheard of by a child. The general question on everyone's mind must have been, "What is this young boy doing and where are his parents?"

But, though he was so young, the Bible says that everyone who heard Him was amazed at His understanding and His answers to their tough questions. After three days, Jesus' parents finally found him. When they chastised Him about not staying with them, He responded by saying, "Why were you searching for me? Didn't you know I had to be in my Father's House?" Little did the Synagogue leaders know that their long-awaited Savior had been among them.

The Savior that was to save them from their problems and their enemies did not come as a Warrior but came as a regular-looking person; and he was focused on saving their Souls instead of their Earthly lives. In God's way, He is more interested in saving our Souls that will last forever in Paradise than physical bodies that will almost always last less than a century.

"What a story," I thought to myself. In all of the books that I had read before, none were as eye opening or more fulfilling. I kept on reading a little at a time to find out what had happened to this boy,

Jesus. As I was reading this great story, I realized that there was a long break in this story in the New Testament. The life of Jesus did not pick up again until he had reached the age of thirty.

Another story within the Bible was unfolding at the same time. There was another man, rugged in appearance, with no Earthly possessions that came on the scene. Ironically, he was Jesus' cousin. He was going around with a loud voice and with a fire in his eye, speaking to anyone that would listen. His name was John the Baptist. He Prophesied that the Messiah was coming in the near future and that they needed to clean up their act. He repeated this message over and over. The Jewish people had heard this story for hundreds of years. They knew that one day their Savior would come, but it always seemed to be "in the future."

To many of the hearers, this scrappy-looking man could not have known anything more than the Synagogue leaders knew. He probably was some lunatic that had basked in the Mediterranean sun too long. This determined man was telling them things that they had heard before, but this time it was with authority. He talked to them about believing in God, following the Ten Commandments, and that the Savior was coming. This wild-looking man was repeating this same message over and over but for some reason it sounded different and more convincing. His message was that the Jewish people were to stop sinning and turn back to God's way.

People were getting off track then, just as now. The sins of those days were probably similar to the ones of today. This man was saying that it was not too late to change from their evil ways. They had to repent of their hatred, their thievery, and their infidelity. These were some of the many sins that derailed them. Just like a train that has gotten off track may inevitably injure or kill the passengers, this man was saying that their sins would injure or kill them. And the same applies to us. If we can break away from doing bad things (like John the Baptist had described), we have a chance at freedom from personal slavery, illness, unhappiness, and discontentment.

Reading what this scrappy but gifted man had to say affected me also. As I was reading his words, I wanted to do what he was talking about rather than simply listen and forget. I knew at this point that there was more to life than just making a living, having a good time and then dying.

John the Baptist was saying that they needed to be Baptized with water. The water was symbolic in that it was a form of Ceremonial cleansing. John wanted to cleanse people of their sins. He knew that the Great Savior would soon arrive and he wanted everyone to get ready. It is the same as if today, we're expecting a special visitor to come to our home. We would clean our houses and straighten up our things in preparation. John was getting everyone ready for the most special of all visitors!

Many people of that time asked John if he was the Messiah that the Old Testament had Prophesied would come. He would humbly reply that he was sent to pave the road for the Great Savior. He said that he would baptize them with water but the one who would be coming would baptize them with the Holy Spirit. This Holy Spirit would be like a continuous, never ending breath of fresh air that would connect God to the individual. What an awesome connection! This connection would last forever. It would free them from their sins and sorrows and they would be ushered into God's Kingdom.

As the people were waiting in line to be baptized with water, an Earth-shattering event was about to happen. The man next in line to be baptized was the Savior of all humanity. The one that John had been saying would eventually arrive was in their very presence! John, the baptizer of the people, was waiting for this moment to happen all of his life. The Savior Jesus, without any public recognition at this point, requested that John Baptize him also. That symbolic moment would change the World forever. What I read was filling me up like nothing else before. Even though I was attending Church, it was more out of habit than anything else. These words seemed to have life in them. They seemed alive...not merely dead, lifeless letters.

According to the BIBLE, Jesus was thirty years old. He would only be on Planet Earth for another three and a half years. Jesus, the Son of God, immediately went around the area that is now the country of Israel, and began to preach and teach of God's Great Kingdom. This was a Kingdom of mercy. God would accept anyone into his Kingdom if they believed in the one great God, the Creator of Heaven, and Earth. This was the story I had heard as a child and as an adult many times over. For some reason though, it made more sense this particular time. I was able to understand it better. Though I did not understand it completely (nor do I to this day), what I did understand was there was a different life out there that a person could choose to follow.

Some accepted Jesus with great joy, but many people viewed him with skepticism and denial. Jesus already knew how people would react. He was not bothered by their skepticism. After all, they were the ones in trouble in their minds and hearts. He knew that those with cold hearts would have a hard time seeing the truth, even if it were right in front of their eyes.

At the beginning of his Mission work, Jesus healed people who had been sick for years and some their whole life. Jesus wanted to set these sick people free from their miseries. Jesus was kind and compassionate to everyone. He talked about caring for each other instead of hating each other. He talked about living forever instead of dying and staying in the ground forever. He talked about hope instead of fear.

His Mission work and life drew me closer to those writings in the Bible. I knew that what I had found was what I had been looking for. Within this phenomenal Book there was no emphasis placed on personal possessions, material goods, being stressed out or "climbing to the top". In this Book of Books there was mention of happiness, peace, salvation, and a life after death that is a life that lasts forever. You don't even have to sign up to be part of this program and there is no annual fee. You don't even have to send any money to someone or donate to an organization. The only thing you have to do is trust the good words and actions of Jesus. Somehow, deep in your heart, you must believe that there is one God who is there for you and me.

"How could this one book help a person feel as though they were worth something and had importance?" I asked myself. I had read so many other books in the past. Most of the books were good, but they were not "filling me up" as I had so desired. At times, they seemed to take me further away from the truth. It became apparent to me that most of those books that I read were merely mumbo-jumbo. These books that I had read were written by man only. They were merely man's interpretation of life. In my opinion, man's interpretation of life without God's guidance and Spirit really does take the form of mumbo-jumbo.

Those who wrote the Bible were wise men and they were instructed by God Himself. Their writings were not designed to be sold for profit; they were designed to teach people how to have a better and happier life. The main Mission of Jesus was to show the World that he was not just a man. He looked like any other person of the times, but was totally different. He was instructed by God to show the Israelites and eventually the World God's great power.

To accomplish this feat, Jesus chose twelve men. These men were to go around with Jesus and watch what he did and said. They were not only chosen to observe, but one day would share what they had experienced with the rest of the World.

Forever in Your Debt

Jesus went all around and taught people that there was a greater power in the World. He only would talk about it, but he showed how powerful God was by healing sick people from disease and afflictions that were impossible to cure. He did this over and over. He wanted to prove to the World that there was a Spirit that mankind could turn to for hope. These twelve followers would watch and learn themselves.

I was getting more and more excited about it all when on a given day, a strange and disturbing thought came to my small mind. I thought to myself, what if this was just a story that I was reading? How would I know for sure if this was just a myth? I was distressed with this thought all day long. I just did not want this to be fiction. I wanted to believe that there was more to life than living and working in a dog-eat-dog World and then just dying. I had looked for the truth for many, many years I did not want all my efforts to be for naught.

That same evening, I was in the middle of preparing something for work that required me to do research. It dawned on me that I believed these textbooks that were written by ordinary men and was not questioning them at all. However, at the same time, there were the books of the BIBLE written by God's men with a wonderful purpose and I was entertaining doubts. This was the last time that I questioned the Scriptures. To this day I might not understand it all, but I continue to believe.

There are Ten Commandments in the Old Testament. However, Jesus added another one that summed them all up. It was to love each other instead of hating each other. According to Jesus, this was not simply a word, but a state of mind and heart.

A good way to start implementing love is to start treating people like you would like to be treated. It does not matter if it is your brother, sister, mother, father, friend, or neighbor. Treat them with respect and dignity and love will be in the air. Telling people that you love them is fine, but telling them that you love them and showing them dignity and respect will carry you a lot further. If we can treat others with love, which is how we want to be treated, a feeling of happiness and contentment is sure to follow.

Jesus showed his love by healing people wherever he went. He healed blind people, sick children, and in one incident, he brought a man back to life that had been dead for several days. There was a lot of love that was flowing out of Jesus. As I was reading this, I thought to myself that this was a person to look up to. This was a person to admire.

Forever in Your Debt

The life and example of Jesus showed me what health, happiness, contentment, and salvation really was all about. Jesus was not just talking about things. He was out doing things. The things he did made people healthier, happier, and more content. And above all, he was offering hope and salvation to anyone that wanted it free for the taking. He wanted nothing for Himself but wanted the people of the World to have all the important things. Just like a good mother would go without something for her child, Jesus gave His all so others could experience health, happiness, and contentment.

These twelve men that Jesus chose were to be witnesses to the great works that God could do. Jesus' Mission was to help people find their way back to God again. Many people had gotten off track in those days and he wanted them to get back on track. He knew that the people in all generations would stray from the truth. He wanted us to be able to know the way we could follow one day. God knows that it is never too late to get back on track. God never wants the Devil to take over His people. God wants us on his side and not on the Devil's side. God wants us to be with Him rather than the Devil for all eternity. God does not want us to just talk a good talk but he wants us to walk a good walk. Just as no good parent wants harm to come to his or her children, God does not want harm to come to us either. I believe that this is why Jesus came to Earth when He did. He focused on getting mankind's minds on track with God again. By His sacrifice, every generation afterwards would have something to follow.

Again, it is never too late to turn your life around. It is never too late to take a different path through life. It is never too late to renew your faith again. No matter how much food or water we drink on a given day, we need to do it again and again. Just because we eat today doesn't mean that we don't have to eat tomorrow.

Our faith is similar. No matter how strong we are as Christians, at any given time in our lives, the Devil will still try to work on us and catch us at a weak moment. Through learning more and more as to why the BIBLE was written, we can use it as a tool to fight off the Devil. This can fertilize our Soul and keep the Devil at bay. The tools needed to keep the Devil at bay are prayer, asking God for strength and treating people around us, as we would like to be treated. We must do this each and every day.

We need to be Christian Warriors by being strong in our faith each day and realizing that we as Christians have an enemy out there. The enemy is not visible as a person, but exists in situations and in people. The Devil, who is the enemy, uses people to create confusion and temptation in our lives. He lures us to do things that we know are not good for our families or us. When we do these things, we are on the Devil's side. Once he has us on his side, there is nothing but personal destruction to follow. We as Christians cannot allow this.

Out of Jesus' great love for us, he allowed something to happen to Himself so that we can be free from the Devil's fear and darkness. From the time Jesus was Baptized by John the Baptist, His great life took a new and forever lasting turn. It was predestined that Jesus would allow a situation to unfold to show the World that there was only one God and that He was the Creator of Heaven and Earth. This God that Jesus talked about was in total control. And if we listen and obey Him, we can have this control in our lives.

God knows that there exists a bad side to life fueled by the Devil. He knows that the devil wants us to suffer. The Devil wants us to be miserable. The Devil wants us to suffer through life and then die without hope. Now, we all know that everyone dies, usually between the ages of 70 and 100 years of age. However, in the Old Testament, it tells of people who lived for literally hundreds of years. Something along the way robbed humans of this longevity.

Jesus was put on this Earth to teach, preach, and to save all mankind from the Devil. He was here to make it so that whether a person physically died at age 18 or even 180, they could have eternal life by being resurrected from the dead. Jesus' Ministry was for only a brief three and a half years. However, the effect He had on mankind is beyond calculating. His love and miracles have given hope to the hopeless. No one had ever done that before.

There was one final supernatural event still to be done to show God's awesome power. Jesus still had to endure suffering and pain. He had to be put to death for the last miracle to happen. By being put to death, it was a kind of death that was not quick. During the time of Jesus, people were executed by being nailed on a big wooden cross. This would assure that the person being killed died a slow, painful death. Jesus knew that he had to die this way.

As I kept reading and trying to understand this Bible book, the problems I had been thinking about didn't seem so big after all. Here was a man that had to suffer a slow and painful death for everyone including me. My desire to find health, happiness, was being fulfilled in a unique way; not by someone speaking answers to me with clear, concise words. But by an inner "knowing", a

"Spiritual knowing", if you will. This was truly exciting to me.

Jesus had warned the twelve Apostles what would happen. He told them that He would be crucified. Crucifixion was the manner of execution in which the criminal was put upon the cross, humiliated, suffered, and died. Those crucified were kept on the cross as long as possible so as to cause a more painful death. Their crucifixions became public spectacles.

Those responsible for Jesus' crucifixion wanted Him to suffer like a common criminal. He told his twelve Apostles that the people that would put him to death were his own people, the Jews. These Jews did not believe He was the Messiah, even though they had seen all of the wonderful miracles that He did. These miracles were not for money, fame, or personal gain, but out of love for the people. These unbelievers could not care less what Jesus did or what they saw. They were full of the Devil's Spirit and wanted to see Jesus suffer. Needless to say, these people thought that they were the ones putting Jesus to death. However, in actuality it was not them at all. They had no such power if God would not have willingly submitted to being crucified, it would never have happened. But, as prophesied hundreds of years earlier, Jesus was to show the World His great power and hope for mankind through being put to death.

My personal life was getting happier, healthier, and more content while I was reading the story of Jesus. Jesus' sufferings did not bring me joy, but it made me "wake up an smell the coffee." I had been sleeping Spiritually for years, and now I was waking up. I began to understand that the solution to my search for health happiness and contentment was not just going to show up one day on its own. Also, I began to realize that just as Jesus and His Apostles were teaching, preaching and helping others, I had to do something similar.

Jesus was taken to where the leader of that particular area lived. This ruler of the area was a man named Pilate. Ruler Pilate was not of Jewish descent but was the leader of the Roman Empire in that area of the World. You see, the Jewish people were ruled by the Roman Empire during that time. Pilate was told (by some of the unbelieving Jewish people) that Jesus was preaching false things; and they arrested him. The arrest took place because Jesus was talking about love, and healing people and was talking of a place called Paradise where everyone was welcome. This threatened the teaching of the Jewish leaders at the time. I was thinking to myself that the people that arrested Him must have had their heads in the sand and earwax in their ears!

After asking Jesus some questions, Pilate determined that Jesus had done nothing wrong. He refused to punish Him with the penalty of death. He gave Jesus back to the Jewish people and said that they should judge Him and that his hands were clean from this ordeal. Somehow, Pilate knew that this teacher named Jesus was special and he did not want His blood on his hands. Jesus knew all along that no matter what was said, His destiny was to go through terrible suffering, just as it was Prophesied in the Holy Scriptures. The unbelieving Jewish people wanted Jesus put to death. Of course, there were also those who wanted Him set free because they knew who He was. The blinded majority had heard of the miracles of Jesus and of His teachings. Many of them had actually seen His great love and power with their own eyes, but they still demanded to have him crucified.

I could not understand how these people could see the miracles that Jesus did and yet condemn Him. However, this was how God was going to show the World His great love and power. Jesus said that after He was put to death that he would rise again in three days. The time finally came that Jesus was put to death. His death came on a wooden cross on top of a hill for all to see. He suffered just as was described in the Bible. He suffered like anyone would if they were nailed to a wooden cross.

When I had been trying to find health, happiness and harmony, nothing else was on my mind. However, those thoughts were the only thing on my mind as I read the story of Jesus. Here was someone who looked like any other human walking around. In reality, however, He was God's only son sent to Earth to help us. He suffered and died for you and me on the cross. It is no wonder that I was no longer wasting my thoughts on myself, and my petty search for answers to life's questions.

Jesus was nailed to the cross and eventually died a horrible human death just as He said He would. Many people that loved Jesus wanted Him to come down from the cross and show the World His power. But it was not Prophetically written to be done in that way.

After Jesus suffered and died, He was brought down from the cross. He was laid to rest in a tomb. This tomb was a hole dug out of the side of a hill. A huge rock was put in front of the tomb so that no one could enter. In addition, there was a guard put outside of the tomb to prevent followers of Jesus from stealing Jesus' body. If there was no body, those who had arranged Jesus' death were afraid that His followers would claim that Jesus had risen from the dead.

After three days, Jesus indeed rose from the dead! Of all the miracles that happened, during Jesus' life, this was the greatest of all. Jesus told His twelve Apostles that after he was put to death He would rise in three days and it happened exactly as He said. This stuff I was reading made me more and more humble. All the mumbo-jumbo I had read in past years about finding health, happiness, and contentment were all now forgotten. My answers were found in those writings in the Bible. The answers were not really "spelled out" however, a feeling of harmony was settling within me. Though I didn't understand it all, what I understood was that there was someone named Jesus that lived a life of teaching, helping and doing wonderful things; and I wanted to be one of his followers. Even though this story and event had taken place two thousand years ago, it seemed to me that It happened only yesterday. My life during that time was transformed. I eagerly read on to see what would happen next in this story about Jesus.

During the era of Jesus' resurrection, His remaining eleven Apostles were in a small house hiding for their lives. They knew that the leaders of the Jewish community that had condemned Him to death were now on the warpath. They knew that they were looking for Jesus' followers to put them to death and rid the World of Jesus' teachings. These eleven men knew that Jesus was the Son of God and they knew not to be afraid. But as can happen to anyone, the Devil sneaks in our hearts when we are weak and makes us fearful.

At the height of their fearful state, a knock was heard at the door. A quiet panic filled their hearts. They were certain that they had been found by the Roman soldiers (who had been sent by the Jewish leaders). They were reluctant to open the door, but knew that if they didn't, it would be broken down anyway. When they opened the door, to their relief a lady named Mary was there. The Bible refers to her as Mary Magdalene. She had done many evil things during her life. She was driven by the Devil and had no hope at all in her life. Jesus restored her Soul and made her a Godly person again. And she was forever grateful for the second chance. After she received her second chance she became a great follower of Jesus.

Interestingly, Mary Magdalene is the person that Jesus appeared to first after He arose from the dead. She told the Apostles in hiding about seeing Jesus alive but they didn't believe her. They thought she was out of her mind. They probably doubted that Jesus would first appear to her rather than them. Or perhaps they thought that Mary was imagining things. Even though their beloved teacher, miracle doer, and Son of God told them exactly what would happen, they still did not believe Mary Magdalene. The fear was fueled by the Devil and reigned in their minds and hearts.

I have personally wrestled with doubts in my life, so I can easily understand how Jesus' Apostles could be temporarily blinded to the truth. It seems to this day that we get blinded. We sometimes do not know what is true and what is imaginary. I just had to keep reading on. An eagerness to read further and learn more overcame me.

After a certain period of time, Jesus appeared to his Apostles in that small house where they had been hiding. The first thing Jesus said to them was, **"Peace be with you. "** He knew how terrified they had been during this whole ordeal. An immediate peace of mind and heart filled them. The Shepherd of their hearts and minds was back like He had promised. What a moving moment this was for me. I imagined myself being in a fearful state and the Spirit of the Lord coming to me and saying, "Peace be with you." What a glorious feeling that would be! I know I wouldn't understand it all, but I sure would welcome it.

The contentment that I had so long yearned for had finally arrived. It was simple and free for the taking. Of all that I had read in the past, nothing was quite like the words of Jesus saying, "Peace be with you." Just as I felt comfort and peace in those words, I knew without a shadow of a doubt that the men chosen to follow Jesus were also immediately comforted and no longer afraid.

An interesting thought came to mind after I read this, and it put things in perspective. I used to watch old Western movies when men were condemned to death by hanging. At the last possible moment, word would come that the hanging was to be halted. What a glorious feeling would come over that condemned man! That man would never be the same again. He had been condemned...but now was spared. He had been bound...but now was free. And what a debt of gratitude he owed the issuer of the pardon! The condemned man would be forever in his Savior's debt.

Jesus' eleven Apostles knew they may have only days to live. But God's awesome power trampled the effects of the death of Jesus. It unlocked the grip of death, hell, and the grave. He now appeared to his Apostles not only to free their mind from fear but also to fulfill the promises He had made. He promised that He would have to die. He promised that He would arise in three days. He promised that we could have eternal life and eternal happiness if we believed Him through the words recorded in his carefully crafted book, the Bible.

After Jesus came to them, they were delivered from fear. They were then instructed to go into all the World and tell anyone that would listen that there was hope through Jesus' example, teachings, and eternal life He offered. God designed mankind in a way that physical death would be eternally vanquished by relying on receiving His eternal Spirit. For whatever reason, the Devil can take our bodies (by physical death). However, if we can remember the story of Jesus' life and believe in Him, we can overcome the Devil and live forever in Paradise.

The good Lord gave good hearts to the Apostles and to all mankind. He gave good hearts to everyone to use as a tool to help each other out. This life can be a little tough; if we don't pool our hearts together, the Devil can make inroads into our Spirits. The good Lord gave us brains also. He did not give us brains just to have, but he gave them to us so we would use them. If He did not want us to use them, He would not have given them to us. He gave us brains so we could make good decisions in our lives. He wants us to use our brains to make decisions that will make ourselves healthier, happier, and more content. If we can make better decisions, we will be able to work less. Then we can spend the extra time to help one another, to have more time with our spouses, to have more time with our children, to have more time with our parents and most importantly, to have time to think of Jesus Christ.

By having time for all of this, we can renew our love for each other and renew our strength in God. And ultimately, all of this will give us strength to fight off the Devil without us even knowing it. Without the tools of a good heart and a good mind, there is no way we can fight against the Devil's wrath. The Apostles were forever in Jesus' debt after He came back to them. Likewise, we can choose to be forever in debt to Jesus. Then and only then can we find health, happiness, and contentment that will last forever.

Chapter Three

WHAT DOES IT MEAN TO BE A CHRISTIAN? HOW TO APPLY CHRISTIANITY TO OUR LIVES

A long time ago when I was a young boy in sixth grade, we decided to go swimming at a neighborhood middle school. There was open swimming at the middle school once a week. As it is today, a person can go with their parents to a pool, pay a fee and jump in. At that particular time in my life, a group of friends and I decided to go swimming without our parents. We put together what we needed and headed off to that neighborhood pool. The middle school pool was shallow at one end and deep at the other.

When I would go to a pool, I would only swim at the shallow end. I did this because I had not taken swimming lessons yet. Neither I nor my friends had ever swam in this particular pool before. We made it to the middle school and went through the procedure of changing and showering. The only thing left to do was jump in. Since I had not been there before, I asked one of my older friends which end was shallow. I simply figured that he was older and that he would know. There was a lifeguard there but though my older friend would surely know as much as the lifeguard. I could have even waited to check out the pool to see which side looked like the shallow end. Instead, eager to jump in, I got a running start and jumped in with both feet, expecting to touch the bottom.

     I quickly realized that there was no bottom to hit! I had jumped directly in the center of the deep end. Not knowing how to swim, I immediately panicked and thrashed my arms around trying to find a wall to hang onto. The lifeguard didn't even see me; who knows where his mind was. After what seemed an eternity of screaming for help, an older child came to my rescue and helped me get to the edge of the pool. I was exhausted and relieved to finally be at the edge of the wall.

     Just like anyone who is drowning and screaming for help, it is paramount that we ask for help from our good Lord. Just as that friend heard me screaming for help and came to my rescue, so will our great Lord come to our aid. Our Lord is merciful and will hear our cry for help. If I had not cried out for help when I was in that pool I would not have had a chance to write this book or do anything else in my life. We must ask for help when we need it. We need to ask help from friends and most important, we need to ask God for help.

I had always thought of myself as a Christian. But only after I started reading the Bible and applying it to my life did I start living the practical Christian life. I didn't just want to refer to myself as a Christian; deep inside I wanted to express it.

If we had close friends and wanted to show them that we really liked them, how would we go about it? We could just keep quiet and keep carrying on as normal or we could verbally tell this friend that we really liked them. We could go the extra step by doing a little something for that person that would show our appreciation for their friendship.

Personally, I wanted to do something extra. In the above case, I used the example of friends. In my case I wanted to do something extra for God. I had this renewed feeling of health, happiness and contentment that God gave me and I wanted to give something back to Him. The first order of business was to acknowledge to God daily that He was in total control. I know that these are just words to the human ear but after reading that Bible, I wanted to continue to believe. I guess I could have chosen not to believe the words of the Bible but it sounded right to me and most of all it gave me hope and comfort. Nothing else really did before, so I reasoned that I shouldn't turn my back on something that helped me so much. As a matter of fact, turning my back on something so wondrous seems hard to imagine. I hope never to even consider it.

The most practical thing to do each day is to read the Bible. I recommend that the Bible be read a little paragraph at a time, rather than pages at a time like a regular book. Personally, I was not in a hurry to finish reading through the Bible, but in a hurry to understand. By doing this, I figured it would please God that I was staying in His words and ways. Also, I thought it would give me support to carry on with my day-to-day living. Just as I found time to feed my belly each day, I found time to read a little bit of the Bible each day to nourish my Soul. Lord knows I would not miss a daily feeding of my stomach; therefore I choose not to miss a day taking in Spiritual food by reading the Bible.

The second thing that I was going to do for God and myself was to not fall for the common teaching that the World was somehow accidentally created in a "big bang". I found it hard to believe that some cosmic explosion was the way mankind came into being. I was taught back then, and still now, that some big bang happened millions of years ago and then all the cosmic dust in the sky somehow organized itself into the wondrous creation we have today. This "accidental organization" somehow made the Planets and certain life forms that turned out to be you and me. This scientific way of explaining things was nice for the science community so that they could understand. However, I chose to believe the Bible's version on how we came to be.

Again, why believe man's thinking? I had tried to believe man's reasoning back when I was looking for the answers to life's questions of health, happiness and contentment. Yet all I came up with were empty answers. When I turned to God's words written in the Bible I found what I was looking for. I was determined not to listen to any scientist but to listen only to God's version of events recorded in the Bible. I reason that if this "big bang" was to have taken place, there would be some kind of life on the Moon or on Mars but there is not. The only life we know of is on Planet Earth. I believe that if there is life somewhere else, God created it, not some cosmic explosion. For whatever reason, God chose to put us on this Planet. By accepting the truth, we can start living according to His plan.

Obviously, believing this truth does not fix all our problems. Awful things still happen to practicing Christians. But now, with this knowledge, we have a tool to fight off the Devil when he gets into our lives. God's love and protection can ward off the Devil. If we don't have a firm belief in God, it is inevitable that the Devil will rob us of what God has intended for us: a full and complete life of health, happiness, and harmony.

To conclude, first of all, we need to ask for help and guidance from God in prayer everyday. Secondly, we need to accept the teachings of the Bible as correct and designed for our own personal good.

These two concepts are absolutely essential if a person is serious about living a Christian life. I often think of these concepts as tools of the trade. We have the tools, but we must put them to use for good to come from it.

In the Bible, there is a passage where Jesus proclaims that he is the Alpha and Omega. This has reference to the letters of the Greek alphabet. Alpha is the first letter of the Greek alphabet and Omega is the last letter. The point here is that God is the beginning of everything and God is at the ending of everything. The "beginning" can signify how our life really "begins" when we come to personally know God. The "ending" can signify how God will be with us to the end of our lives.

To be a practicing Christian, we must have a new starting point. Many years ago my new starting point was to proclaim in my heart and mind that I would be a practical Christian. This means that I surrender my life and heart to God and ask for His guidance every day. I ask for direction, health, and harmony every morning. Also, I say the Lord's Prayer to myself morning, noon, and night. I don't say these words in a vainly repetitious way, but with sincerity.

In Matthew Chapter 6, verses 9-13, Jesus told His Disciples that they should pray like this:

"Our Father who art in Heaven hallowed be your name. Your Kingdom come, your will be done on Earth as it is in Heaven. Give us this day our daily bread and forgive us our trespasses as we forgive those who trespass against us, lead us not into temptation, but delivers us from evil. For thine is the Kingdom and the power and glory forever. Amen."

Jesus taught His Disciples that this was a model prayer. It doesn't take a rocket scientist to know that if these words are chosen by Jesus for his

Disciples, it stands to reason that this prayer is good for us to remember and say daily. Jesus taught his Disciples and followers these words so they could instruct others after he ascended back to Heaven. Jesus' teachings, from which were carefully written down by his Disciples, would be passed from person to person until the end of time. This way, everyone, in each generation could receive God's guidance throughout his or her lifetimes.

Just as Jesus showed his Disciples how to pray and what to say, I decided that I would say this prayer not just once but three times daily. As I mentioned earlier, it was important that I pray regular and systematic. At times, I would get off track and miss one of those daily prayers but always went back to them. Just because I got off track didn't mean that I would stay off track. Being on track seemed practical for me. I wanted to continue being a practical living Christian. Just saying that I was a Christian did not do anything for me. But saying the Lord's Prayer seemed to make everything in my life run a little better and smoother.

At the same time I began using religion as the tool it was meant to be, I was also going to Church. However, I was going just for the sake of going. It wasn't that I was expecting something supernatural at every Church service, but I was going just out of tradition. Also, during that time, I was listening to a few television Evangelists, and reading books on religion. All of this was fine, but often it seemed that the Churches were always focusing on building projects and donations. Meanwhile, the television Evangelists seemed to always be asking for donations.

I was yearning to find a simpler version of religion. Jesus gave the answer to me without any big revelation. It just was obvious to me one day. What did Jesus do in his lifetime? He basically cared for the people. He did this by teaching them about God above, and helping the people with their difficulties. So, since this is what Jesus did, I figured that maybe I would do the same. To be precise, I didn't go around and teach about God but I tried to follow what He told us about God. Instead of going to Church once a week just for the sake of going, I decided to attend Church in my head and heart every single day. Though I often felt that I came up short in my mind and heart, I consciously tried to think of God everyday. By doing this, my days were better and things went smoother.

Though I didn't go around helping people with the same difficulties Jesus did, I tried to be kind and lend a helping hand in any way that I could. I did not talk about these things but just did them. When I started to do this, my life began to hum along a little smoother each day. Just as Jesus lived by example, I also believed that I needed to follow in His footsteps in my very small way. I still believe this today. Though talking about these things is important, being a living testament was the way I thought it should be.

I wanted to follow in the same path as Jesus did whether I was rich or poor. I wanted to be a good follower of Jesus no matter what job I had. I wanted to be treated nicely by people so I treated everyone nicely. In addition to asking for help and guidance everyday, a practical Christian should treat all people with the same dignity and respect that they would like. Whether a person is old or young, whether of a different race or belief, he or she should be treated with kindness, respect, and dignity. There are billions of people on this Planet and a great many of them are not Christians. Whether Christians or not, we are to show Christ's love to them.

Jesus said that He is the way, the truth, and the life. He also said that whoever believes in Him will be in Paradise with him forever. He went on to say that if a man is not born again He couldn't get into Paradise. In John Chapter 3 and Verse 3, Jesus is recorded as saying,

"Verily, verily I say unto you, unless a man is born again, he cannot see the Kingdom of God."

Keep something important in mind. In the years of reading the Bible, never have I ever gotten the impression that non-Christians should be disrespected. Some of the greatest Christians in history were once non-believers and one of them was the Apostle Paul, who wrote over half the New Testament. As Christians, we may sincerely want our non-Christian friends to be born again. Jesus instructed his Disciples to go out unto the World and teach every man the truth. Teaching every person that Jesus is the way, the truth and the life is the most important thing a person should do in his or her lifetime. However, it cannot be done by shoving it down their throats. This Christian teaching is something that they must accept themselves.

We as Christians are obligated to live by example. If we live a life of turmoil or if we do things that we know are not good how can we teach or preach to others? Being a Christian is like climbing Mount Everest. It is extremely difficult to do and takes a very long time. It takes preparation and commitment. Being a practical Christian is not easy. Temptation is at hand every day. Therefore, we have to pray and ask God for help each and every day. Living this way will bring others to Christianity; not just talking about it.

Think for a moment of our example, Jesus Christ. When Jesus was doing his great work here, what if He had lived a wicked, selfish life. What would we have thought of Him today? We need to remember this as we work toward living a life more closely reflecting Jesus' example. You know we are all going to fall short. But if we try our best to believe and treat others with respect, we have a fighting chance.

Mankind seems to have the human trait of taking advantage of people. Being a practical Christian does not mean to be so nice that you allow people to walk all over you. We are not to allow people to take advantage of us. As Christians, we often try to be humble, nice, and trustworthy so much that it is easy to be run over. I believe in being humble, nice, and trustworthy. But I do not believe that we are to allow people to merely take advantage of us.

At the end of our Lord's Prayer, Jesus asked that God would deliver us from evil. Just as there are many people that are wonderful and nice, so there are awful and mean people. As practical Christians, we need to be smart about these things. For example, if we live in a town that has a section known for its danger, should we just trust in God and go through that dangerous part of town at night? Or should we use the brain that God gave us and not go through that section of town? I believe that God can make the worst situation good; but if He did not want us to use our brain, He would have not given us one.

There is nowhere in the Bible that says we should be stupid and not use our common sense. As a matter of fact, He knew that the Devil was so strong that He taught his twelve precious Apostles that they need to walk through life being wise as serpents, but as harmless as doves. As wise as serpents means that we need to be conscious of our surroundings and use our heads to make right calls. Harmless as doves means that we are not to purposely injure or harm anyone. God gave us the tool of the brain to figure things out. No matter how hard we try, we will still make some wrong calls along the way in our lives. But as practical Christians, we can minimize them.

I would like to share with you a personal little story on this above topic. A while back, I was out for a nice summertime jog. Out of nowhere jumped a big dog in front of me. I was startled so badly that it seemed my heart would jump out of my chest. This dog was not only big but also was mean looking and aggressive. Now, I had a dog of my own and knew how nice some dogs could be. However, this particular dog was not one of those nice ones. I quickly looked for a stick and of course could not find one. But what I did find was a handful of rocks that I threw at the dog. This action frightened him and he slowly backed away.

When jogging, a runner needs a change of routine every so often. I had been running for years, and so I had changed routes a number of times. In this case, I changed routes to avoid that dog. A few weeks later, I decided to jog that same route again because it was a beautiful scenic route. I did not want that dog's actions to make me so fearful that I could not enjoy that route's scenery. Needless to say, I had not forgotten my incident with that dog. This time I picked up a big stick when I got closer to that dog's house. Just as before, that mean dog was in his yard, unchained with no fence to hold him in. I was sure hoping that he would stay in his yard this time.

This time at least, I was not startled. My confidence in myself had improved since our previous meeting. My confidence was only elevated because of the big stick now in my hand. As I got closer to the house, I noticed that the dog was not moving at all. I felt a little relieved. I thought to myself that perhaps the owners had gotten an electric fence. The closer I got to the house the more assured I was that everything would be all right this time. I even went so far as to think that the owners had installed an underground electric fence for their mean dog.

The road that I was jogging on that day ran directly in front of the house with the dog. I decided to push my luck and go to the other side of the road nearer to the dog, stick in hand, of course. As I began to cross the road, it was like the wake up call for that dog. He perked up and headed right for me. To my surprise, there was no invisible fence. Before I knew it, that dog was almost upon me. Just by instinct, I swung the stick at him. He backed down for a moment. I also remembered the rocks from the previous encounter. So I quickly picked up some rocks from the ground and once again threw them at him. As before, he backed up and gave me a chance to run the other way. At that time, my main goal was merely to get the heck out of there with both legs and hands attached. I was able to flee unharmed but now I felt that I simply had to do something about it. I was no longer thinking of myself but of a child that would ride past this ferocious Cujo.

When I got home I started thinking things through. I had always tried to be a reasonable man, and now with my renewed feeling of practical religion, I did not want to fly off the handle.

However, I knew the Christian thing was not to just let it slide. I got in my car and drove to that dog owner's house. I stayed in my car for obvious reasons, and beeped the horn loud and long to get the owner's attention. Sure enough, the owner came out and asked what I wanted. In a calm and gentle voice I told him that sometimes I jog past his house and on two different occasions his dog tried to attack me. He was taken aback and was a little upset. I wondered to myself what he was upset about since his dog had attacked me, not him. He told me that he would tie his dog up and apologized for what happened. I left it at that and was hoping that this story was over.

A couple of weeks later I thought about jogging past Cujo's route again. I knew that I probably should skip that route to avoid another incident. I had a few different routes from which I could choose, but it really bothered me not to be able to go down a street that was very nice. I continued on, jogging towards Cujo's house. Of course a stick was in my hand. The closer I got to the house the more I was hoping that Cujo would be tied up and everything was fine. The closer I got to the house it was obvious that the dog was not tied up. Instead of going through the same thing that I went through before I decided to head back. I could feel myself changing from a patient man to an impatient man.

I sat at home deciding what action to take next. I could just drop the issue and change routes on my jog. Or I could call the police or Humane Society. Or I could go over to the guy's house and try to reason with him again. After thinking about it for a while I decided to find his phone number and call him. This time, when I talked to him, I expressed quite clearly that I had all I could take. I told him that if he did not tie up his dog or put up a fence I would take him to court and have a Judge decide what should be done. He did not like the conversation, but I didn't care. I had been patient long enough. Well, guess what happened? He must have gotten the point. Now when I jog past his house the dog is no longer running free. If he had not taken this action, I would have taken him to court. This ultimatum made him take appropriate action. On my part, using common sense and Christian practicality rather than brute force or legal means helped resolve and issue that simply ignoring it would not have resolved.

It is important as Jesus' followers to be practical and put things into perspective. We should practice to develop a nice demeanor towards people and be willing to talk to every kind of person within reason. Just as this statement is true, so is the fact that we should never roll over and be abused by people. We should never "sit there and take it" if someone is treating us like dirt. At the least, we need to simply walk away and avoid the situation. Not all people on Planet Earth are good people. A Christian should be keen and realize a problem and danger before it unfolds so, with God's wisdom, we can avoid as much trouble as possible.

Chapter Four

THE COMPASS

Following God's law is the most important thing people can do for themselves. But it is easy to get off track and confused on what to do or who to believe. Mankind has certainly come a long way in the fields of science, medicine, and technology. This is wonderful, because without the advancement of science we would have much more difficulty in our lives. I feel that it is important for mankind to continuously try to improve the quality of their lives, but not without reliance on our great Lord.

I believe that incorporating faith, hope, love, and yes, technology is the best answer. Understanding that God is the Alpha and Omega keeps us in mental and Spiritual check. It is easy to forget that the Creator of the Heavens and Earth when things are humming along financially. Or on the other side, it is easy to forget Who put us on the Earth when we are lost and in trouble in our lives. You see no one is immune to getting off track. We simply must realize that we can get off track no matter what our situation. And by having this understanding, we can consciously get back on track.

A long while back I had an experience that helped me realize how easy it was to get off track. This particular experience was not a Spiritual directional loss but what would be technically referred to as "physical topographical misdirection." In other words, I got lost! It was this event that really helped me with my belief in religion and getting back on track.

The story goes like this. Quite a few years ago, I was walking in the upper half of the Lower Peninsula of Michigan and somehow I got a little disoriented. The area I was in was a small forest. As any Michiganian can tell you, in that part of the country there are many trees. This disorientation that I was experiencing turned out to be a situation that ended with me becoming totally lost. I had not been to that section of Michigan before and the furthest I had advanced in Boy Scouts was to the level of Cub Scout. And now, as an adult, though I had always tried to be a logical man (taking pride in attention to detail), I was absolutely and completely lost!

For those of you having experienced it, being lost in the woods can be terrifying. How can a grown man put himself in this situation? I thought to myself. Not only was I lost, but I was completely unprepared! I did not have a flashlight nor even matches to light a fire. To top it all off, it was late November; and in Michigan, the shorter daylight hours during that time of year combined with cloud cover makes for bitter coldness.

I continued to find it hard to believe that I had allowed myself to end up in this situation. In my mind, I was trying to find a positive aspect to this predicament. Digging deep, I concluded that I was not going to die. Secondly, I had a compass with me and that I knew the direction of where my car was parked. Third, I remembered the road where my car was parked. I knew that by traveling North, I could get to that road somehow; therefore, I knew I would eventually find my car.

I pulled out my compass while there was still daylight and tried to figure which way North was. Fortunately I purchased this compass a few weeks ago and so it was new and reliable. I liked the way it looked and surely did not think I was to use it anytime soon. I certainly did not think I was going to use it in a dangerous situation. Actually, I had intended to merely use it for fun as I puttered around with my children.

Reasoning to myself, I was quite certain that South was the direction I had traveled after getting out of my car. I simply had to go the opposite way and would eventually hit the road. I turned around to head North, but something inside told me I should use that compass just to confirm my intuition. The compass revealed that North was in a different direction than I had thought. I knew that the compass must have gotten stuck a little, so I shook it to bring it to its senses. It gave me the same reading as before. The needle of the compass pointed in a direction that I was certain was not North.

  Unfortunately, due to the cloudy weather, I could not use the sun to determine East and West. As the day turned to evening, I started getting colder; I thought to myself that I should have purchased a more expensive compass. More and more uneasiness was settling upon me. Even though I knew I was not going to die or anything like that, I still felt extremely concerned. My gut feeling was telling me that North was in one direction; yet the new compass was telling me that North was in a different direction. I was ready to continue finding my way by using my gut feeling when two thoughts passed through my mind. My first thought was to blame myself for getting into this mess; and secondly, I recalled the advice a good friend had once given me in case I ever became lost. This good friend was a much better woodsman than I would ever be. He told me a long time ago that if I ever got lost in the woods, I should rely upon my compass rather than my gut feeling. Though I respected my friend's judgment, at the moment I wanted to listen to my gut feeling.

That late November day was not only getting colder but was starting to turn to night. Reluctantly, I followed the advice that my friend had shared with me. Even though I insisted (in my head) that I should follow my gut-feeling, I finally gave into following the compass reading. I could not stop wishing that I would soon arrive at the road running East and West. I took another compass reading to determine North again. The needle pointed a certain direction and I followed the needle reading. I kept on following the needle for some time, but the new area I was coming into did not look familiar.

Instead of getting more confident, I was getting more nervous. I stopped to take a break. I asked myself what I should do next. I wondered if I should continue to follow that compass that was leading me to areas that were not at all familiar or whether I should follow my gut feeling again. Relying on my friend's advice, I continued to head North as the compass directed. The thought kept coming to mind that I should have purchased a more expensive (and reliable) compass! The reading of the compass was taking me over little hills and across a couple of creeks. Now I knew for sure this compass must be acting up. I was certain that those hills and creeks had not been there!

My uneasiness continued to increase. I began to think that I would have to spend a bitter, cold night in the woods. A feeling of panic came upon me as I reasoned that no one would find me; also I was angry with myself for buying such a cheap compass. Then a small miracle happened! I ended up on a dirt road that was not familiar at all; but it was a road, none-the-less. I was relieved but confused as to how I got there. Which way do I go now! I thought to myself, right or left? It was now dark and there were no house lights anywhere.

I stood there for a few minutes and prayed that God would direct me in the right direction. A feeling came over me that I should go to the right. After walking on that dark, lonely road for a while I saw something very faint in the near distance; I hurried to see what was there. I knew it was not the "boogey man", so I hurried on faster. To my total surprise, I arrived at my car. I couldn't believe it! Not only was it my car but my keys were in my pocket. Half-frozen, I got into the seat and sure enough, the car started right up. The first thing I did was to turn on the heat full blast. The second thing I did (while waiting for the air to turn from cold to warm) was to say a prayer and thank the good Lord

Forever in Your Debt

for taking me from a bad situation to a good situation.

After my prayer (while still thawing out), I kept thinking of my friend's advice. If I would have gone on my gut feeling I would never have made it back to the car, and who knows what might have happened during that long and cold Michigan Winter night? The advice given to me by my friend to use the compass had worked, and the outcome was wonderful! Just as that magnetic compass got me out of trouble and showed me a direction to follow, so it is extremely important to have a Spiritual compass to follow. This Spiritual compass is not to be used to find our way of the woods, but to guide us when we have lost direction in our personal lives. Sometimes it may seem that we have direction, while other times it may seem like we are completely lost. Getting lost in our personal lives can happen easily.

Our Spiritual compass is the writings in the Bible. Part of the teachings of the Bible is that the Lord Jesus Christ will take care of us and that there is a Heaven for all of us to enter after death. Reading these writings and following them will help us when we have lost direction in our lives. Just as it was easy for me to want to go on my "gut feeling" in the dark woods when I was lost, so is it easy for us to want to rely on our "gut feeling" in our lives when we are lost.

Those gifted people who wrote the Bible did so under God's instructions. This was His way of providing a Spiritual compass for when we are lost. These writings in the Bible are not just a story, but are designed for a lifetime of advice. Gut feelings are not necessarily wrong, but should only be followed after reading passages from the Bible and asking for God's help and direction. After this is done, listen to your gut feeling, because that might be the answer you are looking for. Never make an important decision until you read a few passages in the Bible and pray for God's guidance. After doing this, you can rest easy knowing that you have done everything God would want you to do. Then you can let the chips fall where they may because that is what God wants you to do.

We still have a choice though. We can ignore all of this and have a life of personal destruction, a life of discontentment and unhappiness; or we can turn to the advice of our religious forefathers and believe in hope of better things to come. There are specific things we can do to allow God to bless us and bring us contentment instead of discontent. We can turn things around and ask for God's help in prayer. We can be good to our families and ourselves. And we can be good to our friends and our neighbors.

We can find happiness by keeping our lives simpler; we can find happiness by not worrying what our neighbors have and what we don't have. We can find happiness by working to provide for our daily bread. God loves us and He will not turn his back on us. Our agreement with Him should be a Spiritual agreement that we will not turn our backs on Him and His ways. God loves it when we pray. God loves it when we do not abuse our bodies with bad things. God loves it when we help our parents. God loves it when we take care of our children and spend lots of time with them doing simple things. God loves it when we treat our spouse as we would like to be treated by them. God loves it when we treat our friends and neighbors with kindness. If we can focus on the things that God approves, He will bless us with the important things in life.

Though I am not as Spiritually strong as I would like, I know the Master Architect of our World. This Master Architect knows our situation better than we do. It is easy for all of us to get off track. When I get off track, I go back to my Spiritual compass; all Christians need a Spiritual compass. There is a tendency for us to try to figure things out ourselves. This is a trap for us Christians. We need to get away from trying to solve things ourselves. Like the Bible says in Proverbs Chapter 3, verses 5 and 6,

> **"Trust in the Lord with all your heart, and do not rely on your own understanding. In all your ways acknowledge Him and He will direct your paths."**

If we do not use the writings in the Bible as a guide we will without a doubt get misdirected and lost. When we get distressed in our lives, the Devil loves it. When our marriage falls apart, the Devil loves it. When our children go in the wrong direction, the Devil loves it. When we lose our job, the Devil loves it. When we commit suicide because everything has gone wrong, the Devil loves it. However, our Great Savior Jesus, the Son of the living God, wants none of this for His children. He wants us to have total happiness; He wants us to have total contentment; and He wants total health for us. He has given us a heart and a brain to use the Spiritual compass to find our way to Him.

I encourage you to pick up the BIBLE and just slowly start reading it. Start with the New Testament portion first. There is a book called John. John was one of the twelve Apostles that Jesus handpicked himself. Though this particular book was written by John, he was inspired by God Himself! This book is very clear as it pertains to the life and teachings of Jesus. This book of only a few pages really is a compass that will help us renew ourselves. This book reveals in a nutshell who Jesus was and why He came to Earth. Read it a little at a time; read it slowly. Read it many times over; a little bit each time. Read it a little each day. It will guide you each day like a compass.

There is only one small problem. Without you realizing it, the Devil will find ways to prevent you from reading the Bible. The Devil doesn't want you to be content, happy or healthy. So he will put roadblocks in your way to prevent you from reading it. You must knock down his roadblocks and push him out of the way. Be a Christian warrior and resist his temptation. Pick up the BIBLE and read the book of John. This will give you direction and pave a better road for you. If you already read the Bible, encourage others (in a nice way) to also read. If we can all do this, the Devil's power gets weaker and all of our lives get better.

Chapter Five

THE GOLDEN RULE

I would be willing to bet that many readers of this book would not even recognize the title of this chapter. By no means am I suggesting that you are ignorant, but this topic is hardly ever talked about. Why is this so? It certainly is not because it isn't important or because it is old fashioned; I believe it is simply the Devil's work to bring you and me down. Most of our parents would probably know this rule and many of them may have followed it. Today, however, I can guarantee you that hardly anyone follows this rule. It is a rule and it is in "the moral book of life" but it is not enforced.

I would like to share a short personal story with you. When I was younger, I had a habit of speeding while driving. After receiving a few speeding tickets, I decided to cool it; when I made that commitment, I simple slowed down and never got another ticket. When the speed limit says 35 miles an hour, I pretty much stay around that; if the speed limit is 55 miles an hour I do the same. It has become a habit. That rule is not to harass us as drivers, but to hopefully keep us from getting into accidents.

Recently, I visited my birthplace, Greece. I went with my son so he could see and experience some of this culture. While in Greece, traveling around in a car, I quickly noticed that there were speed limit signs posted (like here in America). There was one huge difference, though. Everyone was traveling well over the speed limit. In the country of Greece there are many mountains and many sharp turns. On many roads the difference of being on the road or being in a ravine several thousand feet down is about three feet. In spite of this, people do not feel compelled to go anywhere close to the speed limit. No one enforces the speed limit and no one seems to care. I found out later that the country of Greece has the highest fatality rate in all of Europe. Their excessive speed plus their negligence in enforcing the law account for the high number of people who have died. It has taken the toll on family members who still grieve.

The Golden Rule can either be followed or it can be ignored. If we follow it, there will be fewer personal disappointments and accidents in our lives. I'm not referring to car accidents; I'm referring to accidents of life, like family issues or business issues. If we choose not to follow this rule, we are guaranteed to have more accidents in our personal lives. Our good Lord wants us to follow this rule at all times. The Devil wants us to ignore this rule at all times.

So what is this ageless and timeless rule? It is simple. It is found in the Bible in Matthew, Chapter 7 and verse 12. Jesus Himself said,

"Do unto others as you would have them do unto you."

When I first learned about the Golden Rule I was in my mid-twenties. It made sense to me right away. In this dog-eat-dog World that has been thrust upon us, this rule sometimes does not seem possible to follow. Many parents are mean to their children; and many children are disrespectful to their parents. Many employers treat their employees like dirt and in return the employee pays the boss back by not doing a fair job during the workday.

Many people treat others like garbage, and in return the favor is returned. This attitude continues day after day, month after month, and year after year. During this process, the Devil is in his heyday. Remember that the ultimate goal of the Devil is to see you and me miserable, discontent, and totally stressed out. If he can get you and me on his side the war is won by him and our ultimate resting place will be in his house. His house is a house of unhappiness, his house is a house of unhealthiness; and his house is a house of discontentment. He wants you and me to be in this dismal state on Earth and in eternity side by side with him. However, the good Lord wants the total opposite for you and me.

When I was in my mid-twenties, I made a policy to treat other people like I wanted to be treated. Whether I am at the grocery store talking to a clerk or at a Church talking to a Priest the attitude is the same. God does not play favoritism; he loves us all the same. One of the things that I am sure He likes and approves of is when we treat each other with love and respect. Some people were never treated this way, so they don't know how to treat others with love and respect.

All of this is like the domino theory. I must begin by treating my family in a nice, decent, and fair way; in return my family will do the same. Then, when my family and I treat others that way, it won't take long for things to turn around in our lives and in everyone else's lives. All of this is extremely important because the World has gotten smaller with technology and travel; so almost everything that we do will somehow affect someone else. If we can immediately begin treating others like we would like to be treated, I know without a shadow of a doubt that our lives will get a little better and go smoother.

So what does this mean in the grand scale of things? The obvious result is that we would feel better; crime would go down, families would focus on each other, friends would be closer and ultimately this would please God. Needless to say, this would be to the detriment of the Devil and his evil plans. Almost without us realizing it, God provides us with better things that fill the voids in our lives. While this may not result in us winning the lottery, He gives us something far better: His favor and blessings.

There are times that there might be exceptions to the Golden Rule. For example, we all know that if we come to a red light when driving the rule is to stop. If an ambulance is carrying a dying a person, they are allowed to break this rule. Just like the ambulance driver has to break the rule at times, so do we. A Christian has to know when to stop being nice. If someone is about to rob you, it isn't time to ponder the Golden Rule; instead, you need to think about what to do next. You can let the person rob you; or perhaps you should make an attempt at running away; or you may need to fight back. There are some people who are so possessed by the Devil that there is no reasoning with them.

For another example, if you have a boss that is mean and continually badgering you, you shouldn't just sit there and take it. Perhaps you tried to treat your boss by the Golden Rule many times and it has been disregarded or ignored. In this instance, perhaps you need to confront your boss and simply ask why he (or she) is so mean to you. The other option is to quit the job. The good Lord does not want you miserable.

Mistreating people is not a good thing for you, it is not good for society, and God does not look upon it with favor. Also, treating people like you would want to be treated should not be with an ulterior motive. In other words, we must not treat people with kindness merely with the hope of getting money, favors or special treatment. Sometimes the smallest gesture of kindness and unselfish love is the most important. For example, if you are to meet a friend for lunch at noon and know you will be late, it is a small gesture of kindness to call and let them know. If you can't get a hold of them, call the restaurant and leave a message. Think about it. If you were waiting for a friend, wouldn't you like to know if they were going to be a half-hour late? Things happen when we have appointments with others; the least we can do is be kind and understanding to each other.

Another reason to treat others by the Golden Rule is that it will all come back to you. What does this mean? Let's say you are in a situation where you need a friend's help. If you had treated your friend nicely and respectfully in the past, it is more likely that this friend will respond to your distress call. If you have not been good to your friend I would be willing to bet that your friend might not come to help. Your friend may not say that they don't want to come to your aid, but will likely come up with excuses.

All this is not difficult to understand. Building rapport with someone takes time. Do not take friends for granted. Be honest with your friends, and treat them like gold instead of dirt. You might need your friend's help someday; it could be in a time of happiness or even in time of sorrow.

A perfect place to begin to practice the Golden Rule is with your family. If you noticed, I used the word *practice*. Just as a Physician calls his office a *practice*, so must we use the word *practice* in applying the Golden Rule. A Physician keeps trying to get better with his practice (with no end hopefully); and we can do the same with the Golden Rule concept. The goal is to get better and better at it. The more we try to treat others well the easier it becomes, and things start to get better in our lives.

If you are single, the most obvious place to start practicing the Golden Rule is on your parents. Treat them nicely (just like you would want to be treated). Even if your parents are much older, still treat them with respect. One day, you and I will be much older and how would we like to be treated? It is never too late to mend a relationship. If you are not willing to mend a relationship, you have been completely engulfed by the Devil. He doesn't want you to mend relationships; however, God is pleased when we work diligently toward that end.

If you are married, the most obvious place to start practicing the Golden Rule is your spouse. A good example would be to reflect on how you treated each other when you first met. Most likely, when you first met or dated your spouse, there was excitement in the air. You treated each other kindly and courteously and tried not to offend each other. No doubt, you also were on your best behavior. Going back to that mindset is important. We cannot go back in age, but we can go back in thought. That feeling can be captured again if we try. Treat your spouse today with a few of those things you used to do; a love note, a passionate kiss, a warm and gentle compliment, an unexpected gift, flowers, a surprise getaway, etc. Your spouse will be surprised and greatly appreciate it. And guess what? You will like it too.

As time goes on in our relationships, it is easy to have our love diluted. This diluting, or watering down of our love is exactly what the Devil wants. The Devil wants us to treat our spouse with disrespect and callousness. He wants us to take them for granted. He wants us to have a lukewarm and watered down feeling for them; and he wants our marriages to end in divorce. The more screaming and shouting in a relationship the better the Devil feels. The Devil is your enemy and he wants you and me on his side. The enemy wants to capture you and me. We must be conscious of this and not let the Devil win. Begin treating your spouse like you used to. Have fun, be exciting, be faithful, hold their hand on a summertime walk; do not be boring and complaining; and most important of all, treat them as you would like to be treated.

Many couple's love fizzles out because of economic reasons. This *fizzling out* can happen from not having enough money to do the things they want. The area of personal finances can be a tough issue; it can lead to fighting and arguments. Instead of fight and arguing, try to work together as a team and accomplish some of the stuff that you both want. You shouldn't spend every cent your spouse makes. You wouldn't want your spouse to do that to you, would you? Working together as a team for the betterment of your family is a Godly thing to do; I guarantee you that the Devil does not like it.

Forever in Your Debt

There is the exact opposite to not having enough money for your wants and needs; it is having too much money. Having too much money will put you in the same dilemma as not having enough. I have noticed over the years that when people have an excessive amount of money, they tend not to need their spouses as much. They tend to do things that are destructive to their relationships. Again, it is not them that do this; it is the Devil. The Devil does not want a couple to be happy or united; he wants a big wedge put between them and will stop at no expense toward this end. When the Devil gets in a relationship of a couple, he will soon get in the children's relationships. The Devil does not want a parent to spend lots of time with his children. He will trick the parent into spending time working to provide the child with needless toys, this at the expense of spending time with their child. This is a terrible trap to fall into. The more time you spend trying to get ahead; the more you buy for your children; the more discontentment and lack of love there will be between you.

Deep down inside, the children do not want you to be gone all the time. However, the Devil wants you to be out and about, running here and there. He wants you to think that getting ahead is the answer for you. He wants you to get ahead and buy things for your children to supposedly make them happy. However, children really need time and attention. As a matter of fact, they need lots of time and affection. The more things you get them the more distress will come into your life. Having lots of money is all relative. If you are using your extra money on things that are only material, and you are using your money on destructive things like drinking, smoking, and doing things that perhaps you know that you shouldn't be doing. If so, it will be inevitable that trouble will follow you, there will be a price to be paid for this.

The price will come in the form of discontentment. Discontentment will lead to unhappiness; unhappiness will lead to a destructive lifestyle. You will try to find happiness on the road that you are on, but you will never find it. You will try to find contentment on the road you are on, but you will never seem to attain it. You will try to find a healthy body but will never be satisfied. But beyond all this, God will not look favorably upon putting the love of money ahead of time spent with our children.

The Devil will love it if you turn your back on your children and your family. He will love it if you turn your back on God. Do not try to become rich at the expense of losing your spouse and children. If you were a child again, would you rather go fishing with your dad or would you like your dad to be gone all the time? If you were a child again, would you like to go on a bike ride with your mother or would you rather have her out working all the time to buy you things? Why would you trade your time for toys that your children will only play with for awhile and then toss away soon afterwards?

Children say that they want a lot of things, but what they really want is your time and affection. Just like us adults, they want someone to love and feel that they are wanted. I will guarantee you that the Devil does not want you to love your children; he does not want you to treat your wife and children with love. He wants you to climb up the corporate ladder and keep climbing. The more you climb the less time you have with your family and the less time you will have to spend on things that really matter in life. All of this means that you will never be fulfilled in life. Who wrote the rules of climbing the ladder of success anyway? God never instructed us to be rich in money. He never instructed us to be famous. Jesus once taught that it was easier for a camel to go through the eye of a needle than for a rich man to enter the Kingdom of Heaven. The times are no different now than during Jesus' time. The only thing different is that some time has gone by. The Devil wants us to compare ourselves with our neighbors. He wants us to want what everyone else wants; he wants us to be jealous. The more jealous we are the less happy we will be. This is fuel for the Devil and sadness for our Creator. God does not care what you have, but he cares about you and your family. He already has a place for us, a place in which we will be forever free and happy. God promises his people freedom and happiness. So, what is the point of working and worrying our heads off to get ahead?

It doesn't matter what position you end up in your job. It doesn't matter how much money you have. God wants us to implement the Golden Rule on each other so we will be in tune with everyone around us. This gift of the Golden Rule was given to us by our great Lord. The Golden Rule can be a tool to fight the Devil in our journey through life. Also, you will find that it is impossible for us to find peace of mind without it.

A soldier would never dream of going into battle without his weapons, would he? Yet we're just as defenseless if we do not implement the Golden Rule in our daily battles. It is extremely important to dwell upon the Golden Rule every day. We may often fall a little short in doing things perfectly; but if we don't at least make an effort, we will inevitably get off track, and problems will follow.

The Devil absolutely despises the Golden Rule. It is a huge "thorn in his side" and he will do anything to eliminate us from thinking about it. He will do everything to abolish it from your hearts and minds; he will have you try to change this way of thinking. He will want you to believe that this is an old fashioned way of thinking. He will try to make you think that people in today's World don't have an interest in the Golden Rule. He wants everyone to think that it is every man for himself; that it's a "dog eat dog World".

Always remember that even if no one loves you, you are still loved by God. Always remember that even if everyone loves you God loves you even more.

If things are not really going your way, change your way. Start praying for help each and every day. Immediately begin applying the Golden Rule to everyone you come in contact with. You will see a dramatic change in people if you only smile at them instead of looking stern, mean or mad at them. You will notice that people will start doing things for you if you start doing things for them. You will notice that you will feel better about yourself, and most important of all you will be fighting for something that is worth more than any money or gold you could ever save up for a million lifetimes.

Dr. Nick Dreliozis

Chapter Six

THE TREADMILL

There is no question in my mind that if you start physically exercising you will feel better and take one more step up the ladder to finding health, happiness, and contentment. I know you have heard it a thousand times on television, from your doctor, from a family member, and maybe even from your Priest that exercise is good for you. I can guarantee you one thing; if exercise is a chore for you to do you will not do it. It is as simple as this. Some people like to exercise and some do not. There are many reasons for this; one of them is that some people just simply do not like to do it.

Sometimes we do not like to do certain things however it is important to do things that we do not like to do. One example is our need to go to work everyday. If we do not go to work everyday we will pay a price if we don't. In this instance, the price to pay will be that we will be unable to support ourselves. Secondly, we will not be able to get the things we need or want. Exercise is sort of like going to work. We might not want to at times but we must. We might like to exercise in high school but it seems that when we graduate high school we seem just to put exercise on the "back burner". If most of us continue to exercise after high school, it is only a matter of time that things get in the way. Going to college, getting a job, and getting married are all good reasons to get off track from exercising. It is difficult to exercise when we are tired, and always busy. As a matter of fact, when the workday is done and we come and sit down to a big meal, you might as well kiss exercise goodbye? This is especially true when it is Winter and dark outside.

Personally, I've been exercising all of my life and still, at times I get off track with exercise. Even though it is sometimes difficult to stay on track, I still do it. I might take a break from exercising from time to time, but something inside tells me to just keep at it. All the health experts seem to agree that it is good for us and that it improves our quality of life. It might not be absolutely necessary to lengthen our life spans, but it will likely help prevent many illnesses from coming upon us. Of course, quality of life is more important than longevity.

I remember a period in my life that I took a long break from exercising. I was busy with my job, busy with my wife, and busy with my children. To top it all off, my children had colic and those of you who have had children with colic know that this can rob you of many good nights of sleep to say the least. It is difficult to be happy if you don't get enough sleep; the last thing on your mind will be going out for a jog. During this time when I took a long break from exercising, I began to "not feel well." Even though I absolutely knew I had to start exercising again, I just didn't.

After a few months of taking a break from exercise when things started to settle down I again began to exercise. It was a little hard to start up again. For a while there, I thought maybe I should just stop all together. Something inside again told me not to quit but to go back to what I knew was good for me. I started exercising a little at a time. Nothing too Earth shaking, but just a little to get going. As some of you might know, the hardest part is just to begin. I ran a couple of blocks at the beginning; then I ran a couple more; I just continued this until I was doing enough for myself. Others may be in good enough shape to simply "pick up where they left off" but most of us have to slowly get back on track.

A story that I often remember about myself is when I was eighteen years old. This is the age at which I received my Black Belt certificate. I had been working out in Martial Arts for a long time and now it had been time to test for my Black Belt. After receiving my Black Belt, I worked out in

Forever in Your Debt

Karate about five times a week. Each session of working out ended up going for a longer and longer time period. One hour of working out became 1½ hours.

This was no big deal because while in high school, a person usually has more energy and time. When I went to college that fall, I still continued to work out as before; and now I had to keep up with my college classes. My half-hour workout was now turning into two hours. By the time I finished working out, took a shower, and visited with friends, the time would often stretch 2½ hours!

This schedule continued on for a long while. I was beginning to get tired of the schedule and exercising was becoming a chore. I enjoyed practicing Karate and knew it was good for me. However, I began to reason that I had gone to college for an education, not to spend all my time in a Gym! I quickly realized that this schedule could not be kept up. I took a break from Karate for a couple of weeks. I then began to work out no longer than one hour. This included getting ready to work out, working out and then taking a shower. Instead of focusing on *every* move, punch and kick at each Karate session, I focused on only *one* move, punch, or kick at each session. This decision allowed me to fully concentrate (and nearly perfect) each move without spending a seemingly endless time in the Gym.

What was the point of my working out anyway? First of all, the reason I was practicing karate was that I enjoyed it. Secondly, it was good for my mind. Third, it was good for my body. I was not doing it to become a champ or anything of that sort. After streamlining it to fit my life and my schedule I felt better about it and it did not take all my time. You see, I was working out all those hours because the people I was hanging around with were doing it, so I felt that I should do the same. When you begin an exercise program like walking or jogging, work it into your schedule, not just your friend's schedules. Arrange your exercise program with a friend, but do not exercise at a time that is inconvenient. If you can't come up with a common time to exercise with a friend, do it on your own.

You might have to make hard choices in your life to exercise. A lot of things we do are worthless anyway. Find out the things that eat up your time and cut them out! One of the first things to cut out is watching TV. This is all right to do when you are taking a break or if it is the dead of Winter. But in general, you are not getting anything worthwhile out of it. In essence, you are watching people work. When in high school, I used to watch a lot of TV; however, after high school I pretty much cut it out all together. I needed the extra time to do more productive things like studying and exercising.

After college, I needed the time to work, spend time with my family, do fun things, and exercise. Watching TV was taking up too much of my time; and in return, all I got was a little entertainment, which realistically did not give me anything important. I didn't cut out television altogether but cut it back 95%. I watched it a little so as not to deprive myself entirely. You can also do this. You do not have to do what others do. God wants you and me to have a good chance in this life to be content, healthy, and happy. We need to "rev ourselves up" and do things that we know are good for us and avoid (as much as possible) doing things that are bad for us. I would encourage you today to start exercising. I suggest Mondays, Wednesdays, and Fridays as the best days to exercise.

I would encourage you to begin a jogging program, even if very lightly at the beginning. Perhaps jog just a few minutes at first. Maybe jog slowly for a block and then walk a block. Don't purchase expensive running shoes. You won't be running a marathon. A "middle of the road" (expense-wise) shoe of any decent brand will do. Don't make it a chore. Simply put on your shoes and go! It really does not matter what you wear on top; just do it! After you run for a while you might want to purchase some sweat pants or shorts. Even at this slow pace of jogging, you will feel better physically' you will feel better mentally and you will be more content with yourself. Most of you will be able to jog even if you don't think you can. If for some reason it is impossible for you to jog, ask your doctor for an exercise that will be comparable to jogging. I would encourage you to jog outside if you can. The good fresh air will make you feel better. If possible, I would encourage you to run outside, even in the Winter. That is when most of us need it the most! Of course, if it is too cold or icy do not go outside or you could risk injury.

Maybe you would want to take a break from it during the Winter; or maybe you will choose to run inside somewhere. My suggestion is that you run regularly in the Winter in spite of the coldness. Perhaps you are a senior. Or perhaps you've never exercised before. Well, it is not too late for you. Just do exactly what I mentioned earlier slow and easy and you will be just fine. The worst case is that you just do not want to go outside. In that case, get a treadmill and exercise indoors! Invite a friend over and take turns running on the treadmill. Your friend(s) can come over three times a week, twice a week, or once a week; there are no rules. Whether a friend comes over or not, you get on that thing and go!

Forever in Your Debt

I know God wants us to live a long life. I know God wants us to feel better. I know God wants us to be more content. I know God wants us to be happier. I also know that the Devil wants us to be miserable. He will do everything he can to have you get off track. Follow my suggestions on exercise and you will please yourself, please the people around you and most important please God. No one wants to be around a grumpy person. When you are feeling better, you will be better around other people. I also guarantee that if you exercise and feel better, God will arrange to have things "go your way".

Chapter Seven

TO BE OR NOT TO BE...A COPYCAT

I remember as a young boy an older person offering me a piece of advice that has remained with me my entire life. I am certain that this advice came from his many experiences he had gone through. I can't even remember what prompted this friend (my senior at the time) to share his knowledge with me. I am sure that you have probably heard these wise words over the years. It is simple and to the point. He said to me "Nick, if someone jumps off a cliff, you do not have to follow them."

As I recall I had wanted to do something a friend had done and my older friend cared enough to step in and share those simple but effective words with me. He obviously did not want to sit back and allow me to get "knee-deep" into a situation that I would regret. I listened to him, and over the years I've thought of his advice often and applied it to my life. Sometimes we need to listen to other people if we want to learn something; but if it's not positive or good for us we should not listen. The things that some people do are negative and destructive; they will lead you down a path that is full of more problems.

How would a young person know what is good or not good? How would a young person know whom to trust? Since young people have very little experience, they should rely on the Godly and wise advice of adults. As adults, we must rely on past experience, our "gut feeling" and praying for God's direction. Even if we make a wrong decision, we can "let the chips fall where they may" confidently know that we made the best decision possible.

Do not be fooled; it is easy to make wrong decisions in our lives. If we are going through hard times or are at a low point in our lives it is easier to make a wrong call. Without a doubt, no matter how physically or mentally strong, we can still be vulnerable if the conditions are just right. Even the wisest person will have their moment of self-doubt and misdirection. If we look back in our lives, we will see that many times (and in many situations) we did not know what to do in a particular situation. We might have made a wrong call by simply not knowing; or we might have made a wrong call by someone else's advice. Even if the advice we are given is sincere, it still could be wrong. It would be nice to never make a mistake, but that is next to impossible. Whether we want to admit it or not, we will make many mistakes along life's way; we must be willing to accept that. When we make a wrong call, we may be tempted to say to ourselves, "I knew better than this. How could I have made such a mistake?"

We have to start somewhere to find answers to questions that we do not know. The first place to start looking for answers is in the BIBLE. The words in the Bible won't necessarily jump off the pages and give you the answers to all your questions. However, the Bible may give you an indirect answer. By "indirect" I mean that it might give you comfort in time of trouble, or the answer may come to you when you are walking, or it might just come to you, or you might be directed to a friend that might help you. No matter how you get an answer to your problem or dilemma it really does not matter! The most important thing is that you will receive some kind of answer. Unfortunately, we all get disillusioned from time to time, and looking at words in a book might not sound like it makes sense. However, it is very important; it is a better source of knowledge than you and I could ever come up with!

For example, if you were going to take a test at school, would you go into it blind? What if this test was important and it determined if you were going to graduate? Wouldn't you take it more seriously? What if it was time to renew your driver's license and some of the laws had changed; wouldn't you want to know what the new changes were? What if you needed that license to chauffeur people for your work, would you not want to take it seriously? If these situations I just mentioned are important to study for, why wouldn't the "test of life" be worth studying for?

Study the Bible slowly and in short segments. You do not have to memorize each passage. It is not memory that will help you but understanding the point of a particular topic. In these words of the Bible you will get a direction, and somehow you will be guided into making a better decision for yourself by using the guidance of the scriptures. By doing so, you can also make better decisions for yourself as well as avoid being influenced by others as much.

As Christians, we will make many mistakes. For some reason, most of us cannot find all the answers in the Bible. If that were possible, we Christians would never have any problems. We would never have a down day; we would never be overweight or underweight; we would never be depressed and we wouldn't be stressed out to the degree we are. The main goal of this chapter is to alert you to ways of avoiding mistakes. I am sure you would agree that the fewer mistakes we make the better and easier our lives would be. The more mistakes we make the more stress our lives will have. We need the words of the Bible to help and guide us. Why live a lifetime of distress? Why live a life of being under stress all the time? Yes, it is difficult to understand all the meanings in the Bible and that is the reason why we Christians still have problems. It would be nice to read the Bible "like a cook book", but it simply is not that easy or predictable. However, it does give us a "recipe" for a healthier, happier, and more content life!

The Ten Commandments and Jesus' teaching are clear. You see, the Devil does not want us to understand the Bible' because if we did he could not lure us over to his side. I personally believe that the good Lord wants us to understand (and apply) the Bible. Though I have not found all the answers, I am consciously trying to. As a matter of fact, I am in the same dilemma that you are in. I do not always make the right call. There is no question in my mind that there is always a Spiritual war going on in our minds and hearts daily. The Devil wants us to stop trying to figure things out. He wants us to get tangled up in his web of misery. Our Lord wants to free us from misery and guide us into true freedom and liberty.

We must keep trying to understand the many aspects of life, as well as the good Lord's guidance.

It is not necessary to sit at home ten hours a day on the couch and study the Bible. It makes no sense to do that. That will make you more and more disillusioned and turn into a fanatic. If this happens you will not be good for anyone or anything. For example, our Lord has created us to need water and food everyday. We do not know why he chose to do this but it is a fact that if we do not eat and drink everyday there will be a problem. We need to do this every day. You would certainly agree that food and water are the most important things for us to survive. You might think that love and prayer are just as important and I might agree with you; however, without food and water you might as well forget about living very long on this Planet. If you do not eat and drink you will not be praying or loving too long! If you disagree (which you have the right to do) just go three days without any water or food and you might get the picture!

When we drink water, we drink moderately. When we eat, we eat moderately. We are not supposed to drink a gallon of water in one sitting. Nor are we to sit on the couch and eat all day long. If we did so, our bodies would eventually change (you might know what I mean). Well, this is sort of how we should study the Bible. Just as we eat and drink in moderation, so should we study the Bible. Too much at one time will get us tired of it and confuse us. By studying the Bible a little bit everyday and "getting the point" of each passage everyday, we will make greater progress.

It is practical and wise to do it this way. Do not worry about memorizing the Spiritual roadmap; just get directions! Use this method as your first tool in making decisions. Since we live in a physical World there are times we need to seek advice from people. Believe it or not, there is a right way to ask for advice from people.

In trying to ask questions the right way, we are sometimes in a dilemma. The dilemma is knowing who to ask or who to copy. It is okay to be a "copy cat" if the person you are copying is of sound mind and body. If you see a friend or an acquaintance, and you like the way they do things (or the way they act), copy them. This person would be the person to ask important questions. If they "have their lives together" they will probably give you good advice. If they are merely "a good talker" and their life is not together like you think it should be, don't copy that person.

People are not what they appear to be at times. I have a service-oriented job and people tell me how they really feel in confidence. I can guarantee you, without a shadow of a doubt what seems to glitter is not gold with people most of the time. People may appear a certain way, with their nice Earthly possessions and nice looking things. However, if you could know the inside story, you may find that you know more than they do. In fact, you might even be happier than them. There is a certain general rule of thumb that you should never expect that the richest people are also the saddest and some of the happiest people are the ones that have the least amount of possessions. Do not try to analyze people too much. Everyone has different talents and peculiarities.

If you need advice on raising children don't just pick up a book and start reading. You do not know who is writing that book, and you surely do not know how *their* children turned out. Maybe that author has a great relationship with their children or perhaps it is just terrible. Find a person around you that has raised their children and they have done a good job. Generally speaking, apples fall under the apple tree. Remember that no human is perfect, but try to copy someone that is as close to perfect as possible.

If you are having problems in your marriage do not only go to a counselor; go to a person that you might know who has a good relationship with their spouse. You can learn from other people's mistakes but generally you want the advice of someone that has pieced it together for a long time with their spouse. If you are having financial problems, do not go to someone that has gone bankrupt five times; go to someone that has it right with their finances. Don't expect just anyone to have all the answers but some people have better answers than others do. When you learn something from someone, or if someone goes out of their way to teach you something make sure that you generously repay them. You should certainly thank them at least a couple of times at the minimum. Perhaps you know someone who has shared a lot of information with you. Or perhaps someone has given you valuable advice or shown other kindnesses. Do something for them like buying them a gift. Be sure to let them know that you appreciate their help. Never take people that have helped you along the way for granted. Most people take their friends or teachers for granted. Once they have gotten what they need, they forget about that person until they need them again. It is extremely important to not take advantage of people.

God doesn't want us to copy the behavior and actions of those living lives in opposition to God's guidance. The Devil wants us to be copycats of all people that do bad things and not morally correct things. God wants you to be a copycat of good and morally correct things; this way you can be closer to Him. The Devil wants you to be with him so he can put you on a track of destruction. Again the good Lord wants you to copy the Bible and its heroes.

Forever in Your Debt

Remember that God loves you and wants all of us to be on His winning team. He will love us even if no one else does.

Chapter Eight

DO NOT BE A SLAVE

No matter where you live on this Earth, fundamental principles for life are all the same. A person needs water, food, shelter, clothing and love to survive physically and mentally. Our great Lord left us a prayer we are to repeat every day so that we may have our needs met. Though the Lord knows we need these things, He wants us to ask for these things. He would have not left it for us if it wasn't important to Him. In the Lord's Prayer, we were instructed to ask God for our daily bread. This has a two-fold meaning. Of course, the first meaning is that we shouldn't take the food we need to survive on for granted. The second meaning is our need of "Spiritual bread" on a daily basis; this is the bread the heart needs to be happy. This "Spiritual bread" is the bread that the Devil wants to rob from you and me.

Without a shadow of a doubt, I'm convinced that the less happy you are, the less healthy you will be and the less content you will feel. When you and I go on a downhill spiral the Devil is in his glory. Being from a Greek descent, there is a part of my past that I often think about. It is a thought that is not pleasant to think about, but it is of a time that the Greek people were slaves to another group of people for four hundred years. Many of them were born into slavery and died in slavery. They had to take commands from someone they likely despised; and their slave masters likely had little regard for them. I also think about the African Americans who were once slaves in America. No slave wanted this kind of life or deserved it. To be in a "slave state" someone has to take over all of your possessions and tells you what to do. What an awful existence this would be. At least in the World that we live in there is not this kind of slavery anymore. After all, who would want a taskmaster over their head telling them what to do all the time? Standing up for basic human rights was futile because they were nonexistent.

Believe it or not, we still have slavery in the World today. The rules or conditions of the physical slavery have changed. This new kind of slavery has entrapped our minds and has taken over our way of life. We are slaves to a situation here in America that we cannot easily see. I believe that this slavery takes the form of believing that we need more than our daily bread to be happy! In America, there is a lot of land, a lot of natural resources, and an abundance of everything! Since there is plenty, people can simply purchase anything they want.

This similarity to modern slavery really comes to light when economic conditions prevent people from purchasing what they want. It seems that we either want what our neighbors have or what is advertised on TV. We want more and more regardless of how much we have. If we have a nice car, we want another, even if the one we have is running well and still looks fine.

Another thing that we want is to go on bigger and better trips; eventually we will never feel satisfied. The story never ends. The more we have the more we want. To get all of this stuff we have to do something that brings in money. Most of us will work in our regular jobs, work overtime, work weekends, work holidays and anything else to get the money. Others might be in a stressful job that they don't really like; but they keep doing it until they retire so they might keep up with their lifestyle. Others might do illegal things just for the sake of getting ahead. All of this is done because something inside our brain tells us to do this. I believe the cause of this is a subconscious suggestion that was put there by observing what others do and visually seeing advertisements.

Here's the scenario. Our good Lord does not want us to suffer and go without. It does not make any sense to deprive ourselves from things that we really want or need. As technology advances and new discoveries are made, our lifestyles become healthier and more comfortable. It only makes sense to obtain these things. These new things cost money to buy, but if it helps you feel better physically or helps in saving your life well it is all worth it.

Here's a potential problem with this scenario. People can end up too busy trying to make more money for things that they **do not need**. Sometimes we think we need certain things but in actuality we do not. It is very easy to get caught up in the mindset that you just do not have enough and one day you will have enough money and be able to just sit back and relax. That day will come and time will have past. The Devil wants you to feel as though you have to get ahead and provide more and more for your family. He wants you to "keep up with the Jones". He wants you to spend time away from your family. As a matter of fact, the Devil thrives on seeing you make lots of money while your family structure crumbles. Often I hear of mothers and fathers placing their careers and jobs ahead of spending quality time with their families. It would be one thing if the items being sacrificed for were the bare necessities. However, usually it is for senseless toys and foolish pleasures.

You see, extra stuff doesn't bring happiness at all. As a matter of fact, it can bring arguments and a lack of appreciation for things that really matter in life. If a person receives a continuous stream of gadgets and toys, (regardless if it is your spouse, children or even friends) they will eventually take things for granted. As a matter of fact, the "receiver" of these goods can eventually lack appreciation for the "giver". Also, the more items you give to yourself, the more you will want. The more trinkets you give your spouse the more that they will want. The more you give your child the more that they will want. The more you give to a friend the more they will want. When this "spoiling" gets entrenched in you (or others) the time may come when "the party is over". Indeed, the time may come when the free flow of money dries up. In this instance, the many toys and goodies will be forgotten; a fear that "the accustomed way of life may be over" takes hold; the very ones who had been loaded down with tons of senseless plastics, metals, glass and wood will not regard you any higher.

At this point you will feel stressed out. You will feel like everything is crumbling around you. At this state you will not ever have a prayer of being content, healthy, or happy. When this state of distress hits you there will be a lot of yelling, arguing, and who knows what else. I know without a doubt that there will be discontentment in yourself and in your family if you constantly work for things that you want. You will never feel satisfied; you will lose your purpose in life. To "lessen the pain" of being in this distressed condition, people usually start doing things that are not good for them. They might resort to drinking, smoking or taking drugs to relieve some of the stress. Or perhaps they will partake of these bad habit-leading behaviors to "temporarily forget about" the situation they are in. This will continue and have a domino effect. One wrong move will lead to another until it is naturally stopped by something really bad happening. The bad thing could start just with a lot of arguing in a family all the time and lead to family abuse, divorce, jail or prison.

During this distressful state the Devil will attempt to keep you on this destructive path. The more destructive the path, the more pleased he is. The more discontentment the better for him; the less healthy you become the more pleased he is; the more pain you endure, the more glad it makes the Devil. I am telling you without a doubt that this cycle can be reversed. It is difficult to do but can be done. The first thing you need to do is to write down the things you need in order to survive. Remember to write down not what you might think you need but what you actually need. A person who does not have very many goods may not be able to cut many things out; but a person with a lot of money and goods might be able to cut out a lot more.

    As you might have gathered by now, I firmly believe that the mission statement for all Christians should be to get closer to the Spirit who has created the Heavens and the Earth. To us, this is God Himself. Second on the priority scale should be to find health, happiness, and contentment. These two extremely important issues cannot be found if we are constantly working and spending time away from our families. God wants us to pray and ask for help; the Devil doesn't want us to do that. Though God wants us to be healthy, happy, and content, the Devil wants no part of this.

    To refocus on the important things in your life, the first thing to do is to unplug your TV set for at least one week. I know this may seem next to impossible, but it can be done! You will see things much differently by doing this. First of all, you will not see what everyone else is doing or whatever everyone else has. You will not see everyone in Hollywood having a good time while you are "stuck in your own little World." You will not see all the fancy clothes and the snazzy cars. All of that stuff that you have been drooling over had not helped you at all (nor can it help)! As a matter of fact, such covetousness could be destroying you and your family. Without you and I realizing it, it can get into your mind and control your thinking.

If you really want all of that stuff, you will have to work harder for it. If you happen to work for someone, you may have to work more hours to get the things you want. If you have your own business, you may have to make tough choices or put in longer hours to have the things you want. All of this will require that you and your mind will be somewhere else instead on your family and thinking of God.

In another situation, perhaps you do not have a decent job. In this instance, you may find yourself sitting home all of the time being miserable; miserable because you cannot get the things that you want; miserable because everyone else has things that you don't. All of this is not the work of our good Lord; it is the influence of the Devil. The Devil is working overtime. He wants you to work all the time or stay home and be depressed. You can fight all of this by remembering what a Christian is. A Christian is someone who believes the story of Jesus, what He represented and did. We must put the views, beliefs and words of others on the back burner and focus on Jesus' views, beliefs and words. Jesus spoke of salvation and eternal life through believing in Him. The Devil merely will rob us from our physical lives (when we die); but

God's people will come alive again in the permanent, perfect place of Paradise.

Jesus did not accumulate Earthly possessions; He did not go out working all the time to buy the clothes on His back; and He sure didn't care about his mode of transportation when He entered the city of Jerusalem. His message was that you and I can find peace with God and find our place in future eternal home free from sorrow, pain, or worry. He never talked about keeping up with the Jones'. He also did not say to just hang around and do nothing. When he preached and taught, He would often stay at different people's homes. The homes He stayed in were merely designed to be shelters from the elements. The bread that those families shared with Jesus was bread that they likely had to make themselves. In many instances, the people of those days had their own wheat, barely or oat fields. Indeed they may have worked in a landlord's field, but the fact remains that they had to work for it. They wanted to share their food with Jesus. Jesus offered them a life that they never had known before; a brand new life filled with promise and hope; a life that would not end when they died, but a life that would last forever. Jesus accepted this bread in respect for the family taking him in.

He could have created his own bread by performing a miracle but he chose to honor the family that he was staying with. All the people he graced with his presence were like his own children; what father wants to offend his child? A good father only wants the best for his children. He wants them to be happy and free from the Devil. Jesus was like their father; he wanted to show them that no matter who they were or where they lived, they all had the same chance of getting to Heaven. Jesus loved everyone. He especially loved the poor and sick at heart. He knew their pain and knew of a way to set them free. He knew that people in pain and with heartache prayed and thought about God more than those with no hurts or concerns.

People with a lot of money do not seem to need prayer as much. They think they can make it on their own. He knew this so well that in one of the teachings he said it was easier for a camel to go through an eye of a needle than for a rich man to get into Heaven. Jesus did not say these things to imply that the rich couldn't get into Heaven; he merely wanted to warn us that wealth could make us "too big for our britches." When a person gets a lot of money, their mind gets focused on things that are money-related. They start to think of better cars, more expensive vacations and a fat-cat retirement. Without knowing it, they can allow money to guide them instead of God's will. I believe that there is a place "in the middle" that will provide contentment.

Finding this "middle zone" Is not that difficult if you always are conscious of two things.

    Before I tell you these things, I'd like to tell you a story that has helped me avoid many mistakes. It is a story of an older man who had a real good job. He also made a lot of money. In the years that he was working he was always under pressure. He worked a lot to get the things he wanted and needed. He also worked to save for retirement and the golden years that were sure to follow. After years of working, this gentleman retired at age sixty-five. Shortly after he retired he developed a health condition and was laid up in bed for the longest time. While lying in bed he was really heartbroken. He was not only heartbroken because he was ill in bed, but he was heartbroken that he never took time to be with his wife and children. He never took time to smell the roses along the way. Even the idea of enjoying life was silly for him. His goal was to work hard when he was young and take it easy later. Lying in bed, and at the sunset of his life, he regretted the decisions he'd made in life.

    Taking time to visit with his wife; taking time to play with his kids; taking time to smell the roses along the way took on a new meaning now. Though some have said, "It is never too late to change your life" it didn't apply here. This man passed away

Forever in Your Debt

shortly after his retirement. To this day, I don't know if he chose the path that lead to Heaven. Being in a service-oriented business, I have never heard an older person say that they spent too much time with their family and friends. They always say the opposite "I wish I would have spent more time with my family and friends."

So the first thing to consciously be aware of everyday is that we will not be here forever. We will have to leave this life that we know and have grown accustomed to. We do not like to think about this, but it is a reality; the sooner we address this reality, the easier it will be. By understanding this principal, and fact we can change our life accordingly. We can understand that no matter how many goods we accumulate, it will not help us get into the Kingdom of Heaven any easier. If we can understand this, we should ask ourselves why we sweat about life's little things. We can take a little easier approach and work for a living without stressing ourselves out to a point where life is no fun. There can be a balance between work and taking the time to smell the roses. You will find contentment if you do this. You will find contentment if you go fishing with your children. If you do a lot of little fun things along the way throughout your life you will find contentment; and you will not have to slave away to obtain Earthly possessions that will merely perish over time.

Instead of doing things for yourself, why not do things for your spouse also? The key word here is "doing", not "buying". Focus on doing things with your spouse that does not cost money.

Jesus promised us a place in Paradise that is free from worry and work. I know that is not 100% possible here, but we can think about it a little and try to start doing it here. Most of us cannot stop working for a living (or even stop worrying) entirely. However, we might try cutting back a little on both. When we do this, we should then try to think about the next life. It is certain to arrive; we can prepare for it by praying everyday for God's direction, showing kindness to others as much as possible. It is also extremely important to start doing things with your loved ones. Unless you are on your deathbed, this still can be done for most of us. Do not wait until you are financially sound to do the little things in life that really count. Do not listen to people who say it is "quality time" that counts. This is merely an excuse for not spending any time with loved ones. Forget trying to find that quality moment and just do things with your spouse, friends or children. If you are a grandparent, spend time with your children and grandchildren. Oftentimes, grandparents spend time with their grandchildren because they did not have time to spend with their own children. Though this is commendable, I still believe you should spend time with your own children as well. I guarantee that your own children need you more psychologically than your grandchildren, regardless of their age. You might be a little older now, but you can change; try to make up some of those years and memories that you lost in your lifetime.

God loves us all the same, no matter who we are. But if you go the extra step in thinking of God and the next life (in addition to spending time with your friends and family) God will love this even more. You will begin to feel a little happier. It will be the beginning to a happiness that money cannot buy. Just as much that God will approve of this, I can guarantee you that the Devil will hate you for doing this. You will have to decide whose approval you want: God's or the Devil's.

In conclusion of this chapter, I encourage you to work and be productive in everything you do, but not to be obsessed with the riches of the World. We might be far richer in our personal relationships and personal growth than anyone on Earth with a fancy car and fat bank account. Most people don't realize this though. I urge you not to "miss the train" that is traveling to the KINGDOM of Heaven. The time is at hand for us to board. Ask God for help daily; be good to yourself; be good to your spouse; be loving and patient with your children; and be good to your parents. By doing God's will, I am certain that God will hold that train to Heaven for us until we can get aboard!

Chapter Nine

GET READY

One of my favorite stories as a child was the story of Paul Revere. His fast and famous horse ride warning the American Colonists that the British were coming was exciting to me! I am sure that most every child in America had heard this story. Mr. Revere's fast and furious ride to warn his people was done because he cared and loved his countrymen. He knew that if he was not able to warn them in time, many of his fellow citizens might be killed. He had to warn his countrymen about the coming danger.

This story has always inspired me; it reminds me to always be ready. Needless to say, I don't need to be ready for a British invasion! I must be ready for something even bigger. It is a reminder to me to prepare for Jesus' return to Earth, as the Bible says. I do not have to get my weapons ready nor my armor. I have to get ready for His approval. This preparation is not out of fear, but out of respect for the King of Kings. I want to follow the teachings of the Bible. When He returns to Earth (and I truly believe He will), I want to be able to say to Him, "I have fallen short but I consciously tried. I am sure I have sinned along the way but I admit it and ask for your forgiveness."

Many have speculated on when his coming will be, and a great many are still speculating. I have never put much stock on what Church leaders (or the laity) have said; their predictions are merely mortal…not divine. People have been predicting the Second Coming of Jesus Christ since he returned to Heaven two thousands years ago. Every time there is a natural disaster or war, people jump up and cite chapters and verses describing, "end time prophecies" and predict that Jesus is coming back soon. My observation is that when people say those words, they usually speak out of fear, not joy and relief. When Jesus chooses to return, it will be on His own timetable. Whether He comes as soon as right now or as late as two centuries from now, His timing is His not ours! Our goal must be to stay steadfast with our faith, and have a ton of patience. We must be the best Christians we can be; and believing in the Bible, we must choose to also get ready for the Second Coming of Christ.

We don't know for certain exactly what Jesus has in store for us. One thing I know is that He would want us to do good things instead of bad. He wants us to take care of our spouses; He wants us to take care of our children; He wants us to treat everyone by the principles espoused in the Golden Rule. He wants us to ask Him for help each and every day. He wants us to be happy, hopeful and to join Him for eternity. The one thing that he does not want is to lose us to the Devil. Therefore, He wants us to prepare for His Second Coming.

Let's look at it another way. In our lives, we prepare for things all the time. If a child plays soccer, he needs to prepare his gear before starting the match. If the child forgets to prepare properly, the parents usually will do so. If, for example, the child forgets his cleats, he will not be allowed to play. He will simply have to sit out the match. Another thing children have to prepare for is spelling tests at school. Simply put, if they do not prepare they will not get a good grade! In the long run, one particular test will not make or break them; what will break them is not learning the concept of preparation.

As adults, we also prepare for many things in life. We prepare what we might wear to work on a given day. We need to prepare what we might have for dinner. Whether we are cooking at home or going out we still are preparing. We prepare on making a decision on where to go for a vacation, and what to take along. Preparation is part of our lives and if we don't prepare, things do not get done without preparation, things don't run smoothly. Let's go back to the dinner preparation example. This is what every adult thinks about. We certainly don't want to miss a meal do we?

Let's use a holiday example. Let's say that it is a few days until Christmas. This year you are planning to not only have your family over, but also your boss and his wife. Your boss is new to the area and does not have family. He is a kind and generous man. He makes certain that your time at work is pleasant. He is understanding when your baby is sick and will give you the time off from work with no hassles. It is three days before Christmas now; you know you have a lot to do if you want the house to look nice and have a nice dinner prepared. Wishfully, you say to yourself that you have plenty of time and you will somehow get it all done. The days pass by and you have still not cleaned the house nor prepared for the Christmas dinner.

The day has come. It is Christmas Day; the house is still not clean and the dinner is not prepared. What a desperate situation! The boss that gives you the check for working at his place of business is on his way over and you are totally unprepared. Would you ever dream of doing this to your family or guests? Of course you would do the opposite. You knew that Christmas day was coming. You knew that your family was coming, and you knew that your boss was coming. All of this basic information automatically registers in your mind; you would prepare your home out of respect for your company. Also, you would have prepared a nice meal to the best of your ability. So, maybe you would agree that this would be an accurate assumption. It is not that difficult. You know how to read a calendar. The month is December. Each and every day gets closer to Christmas. By assembling all of this information, you would calculate in your mind how much time needed to accomplish everything; you would get it done even if you were exhausted at the end (like we often get during that time of year). Nevertheless, the job would get done.

    Preparing the Second Coming of Christ is similar to preparing for that Christmas dinner. It is easy to prepare for Christmas dinner from year to year because everyone knows the date. Even saying the words, "December 25th" and you know it is Christmas! However, the big dilemma here is that we don't know the exact date when Jesus will come back. It is not as easy as knowing that Christmas is on December 25th. Religious leaders and regular parishioners have predicted (with varying dates) when Jesus will come again for two thousand years now. Over the past two centuries, there have been more predictions regarding this issue than over the previous 1800 years combined! Over the past two generations, many religious leader and parishioners have predicted the Second Coming of Christ. One religious sect claims, to this day, that Christ actually returned to Earth (Spiritually) in fulfilling many Biblical prophecies. During World War II, Christ was sure to return due to the great pain, suffering and death endured by so many millions. During the Vietnam War, the same held true.

You may recall where you were when you heard about the terrorist hijacking attack on New York's World Trade Center and the Pentagon on September 11, 2001. I certainly remember where I was and what I was doing. Over 6,000 people were killed. The references to the scripture speaking about "wars and rumors of wars" in the New Testament were rampant shortly after that tragic event. But those who claim that certain ancient scriptures are being fulfilled by present day events apply these views to both major and minor events. Any violence occurring, even in small towns, can elicit claims that these are the "signs of the times." Every prediction over the past two centuries (including our generation) that I've read about has been wrong. Jesus has not come back. All those were mere words and speculations. Do not believe any one of these predictions. We should not set up ourselves for failure by predicting the time of His return. Once you start predicting such things, you are going to be disappointed, and that will affect everyone around you. The truth is that none of us know when Jesus will be coming back. It could be as soon as right now or it could be three millenniums from now. As Jesus said in the New Testament book of Matthew, Chapter 24, verse 36,

> **"But of that day and hour knows no man, not the Angels of Heaven, but my Father only."**

Regarding the same topic, Jesus said in the book of Mark, Chapter 13, verse 33,

> **"Take heed, watch and pray: for you know not when the time is."**

What then does this mean for you and me living in today's World? I will answer that by telling you another one of my favorite stories in the Bible. It is the story about the Israelites and their release from slavery from the Egyptians. Moses, God's chosen person, was sent to Egypt to set God's people free from slavery. Moses had to perform miracles so that the Pharaoh and the Egyptians would fear God and set them free.

In my simplified version, the story continues like this. When the Israelites were freed and on their way out of Egypt, they temporarily stopped their trek near the foothills of a mountain. This was a significant resting point because it was chosen by God Himself. This resting spot was the place that Moses was to receive instructions on what to do with God's people; he was also to receive instructions as to the laws the Israelites were to follow now that they were free. Moses was instructed to climb Mount Sinai so that God could reveal these things to him. The Israelites were to wait at the base of the mountain until Moses came back. Now, remember, this was the same Moses that had performed many miracles; this was the same Moses that had great faith in God and loved His people, the Israelites. Calling Moses to come up Mount Sinai would not only affect His people but would affect all of mankind who chose to listen and obey. When going up the mountain, everyone thought that he would go up for a short while and then come back with some great news from God. Keep in mind, there was no water or food on that mountain. He was supposed to come right back. As the days passed, Moses did not come back down. Three days went by. Four days went by. Five days passed, and then a week. Surely something was wrong. The Israelites were getting impatient. What were they to do? I often think what would you and I do if we were in that predicament. Moses has a brother in the crowd. He knew without a shadow of a doubt that Moses was God's chosen man to help the Israelites. He knew that everything would be alright. He tried to comfort the people and calm them down. He knew the Devil was trying to discourage them with his tool of fear. He assured them again and again that Moses would come back down from the mountain. But the crowd was getting more and more doubtful and anxious. Four weeks had gone by. This was the same crowd that had been patient for four hundred years of slavery. Now they were waiting for a few weeks and they were impatient.

What was taking Moses so long? Surely he was dead. Certainly, no man could go weeks without water and food. They were not sure anymore why Moses went up that mountain. These thoughts of fear and impatience were fueled by the Devil himself. Just like us today, some of the Israelites were more patient more than others. There were some that wanted to wait for Moses no matter how long it took. There was another segment that could wait no longer. They went to Moses' brother (who was named Aaron) and asked him what they should do.

Aaron said that God had delivered them from the claws of slavery after such a long time. We should be patient and wait, just like them. A certain percentage of them still continued to be faithful and decided to continue waiting. The others were getting more and more anxious. This group knew that Moses was dead and they were left alone in the wilderness to fend for themselves. This same group wanted to go back to Egypt. They wanted to go back to Pharaoh. They wanted to go back to slavery. All of this was bad, but in their minds it is better than aimlessly roaming in the wilderness with barely anything to eat.

The days continued to pass by, and now it was closing in on forty days. Almost forty days had come and gone, yet there was still no sign of Moses. By now, a great many of the people were ready to riot! Surely, no man could live on that barren mountain this long. They did not want to hear what Aaron had to say anymore. They forced him to make an idol statue out of gold. Their intention was to have him create this idol statue so they could pray to it. Also, they would somehow find their way back to Egypt and back to slavery. Perhaps they thought they could give this as a gift to Egypt's Pharaoh. Their fears were now controlling them. Their fears would take them back to brutal slavery. Their fears would take them back to tremendous hardship; their fears would force them to turn their backs on the man who, with God's direction, had taken them out of four hundred years of slavery.

What would we have done? Would we have gone back to the Pharaoh or would we have waited for Moses? Of course, we could never know the answer to this question but we can speculate. Aaron, in distress, helped the Israelites put together this graven image made out of gold. They collected the gold from Israelite's jewelry. Even faithful ones that wanted to wait for Moses may have been forced to give up their jewelry. If they would not have given it, perhaps they would have been threatened or killed.

Eventually, the final product was made. It was a golden calf. This golden calf was what they were going to put their faith in. Throughout all of this they had abandoned their Godly ways. They had begun to get drunk and fornicate. It was totally getting out of control in a very short time they had gone from being Godly people to people driven by the negative side of life. Their leader was no longer Moses. Their leader was the Devil, and they did not even know it. These good people (who were turning bad) didn't know the price they would have to pay for this bad decision.

Moses was still up on the mountain. He was alive and well, waiting for God to direct him and his people. Up on the mountain, there was something ready to happen that would change people for generations to come. Moses was God's messenger, and without God's direction, he had nothing to tell his people. After forty long days and nights, Moses was awakened from his stupor by God's awesome voice. God spoke to the steadfast, but exhausted Moses. The mountain around him began to rumble, the clouds darkened and the World was never the same. It was at this moment that Moses and the Israelites had been waiting for. This is the moment that God chose to give mankind his laws. Moses was the chosen one to receive the laws that mankind was to forever follow. This was it...the wake up call! The Great Creator of the Heavens and the Earth was speaking in human words for us to understand. The Alpha and Omega, referred to in the New Testament was speaking to Moses in the Old Testament! Without a doubt, God himself did not want us to speculate anymore about what the ones actually were or where they were drawn. The Supreme Lawgiver was giving Moses the inside scoop. He was being given the guidance from the One who was the Establisher of All Justice. The laws were clear and there was no "mumbo jumbo" in them.

The mountain began to shake and tremble even more. It shook, not out of fear but from the awesome energy in God's message. It was like a rocket taking off for space. A great deal of noise was heard and vibrations were felt. As powerful as this was, God's message was but infinitely greater. The people knew something great was happening. Those who believed that God hadn't forsaken them were filled with incalculable hope. The ones who had turned their backs on Moses and God also knew God was at hand but were filled with incalculable fear. These people knew that they had turned their backs on our great Lord. They had allowed the Devil to rule over them. The ones that were steadfast not only were hopeful but were forever grateful to know that God had them in His plan.

Moses came down from the mountain with God's laws written on stone slabs. God had forewarned Moses that a great many of his people had gone astray. When Moses actually witnessed the debauchery and wickedness of the Israelites, he was saddened and angry that they could not have waited for him. He had, with God's guidance delivered every one of them out of four hundred years of slavery; and yet to wait on God for forty days was too much for them! His heart was filled with both disgust and anger at God's people. Moses was so enraged that he threw the slabs with the ten laws written on them against the side of Mount Sinai. When doing this, the ground opened up and swallowed literally thousands of the wicked ones.

Just like Moses came back to his people with God's laws in hand, so must we wait for our Savior, Jesus, to come back. It has now been around two thousand years since Jesus physically walked on the Earth. This thing we call "time" really is relative. What is the difference between two days, two months, two years, two hundred years, or two thousand years? It is only "time". Sure, there are different people living now than there were two thousand years ago. A hundred years from now, there will be entirely different people living here now. What all this means is that we need to immediately start preparing for the Second Coming of Jesus Christ. Of course, we do not know when he will come…just as Moses did not know when God would speak to him; but he will return, just as he promised. He promised in the New Testament that he would come again one day.

As Christians, we believe that the writings in the Bible are true and good for us; we must believe the entirety of the scriptures. We cannot "pick and choose" what verses we want to fit into our lives, and reject others. I have personally passed down to my children my strong belief that Jesus will come again. At one point in teaching my children, one of them asked me if Jesus would come back in his lifetime. The question was easy enough to answer. Just as his question was basic so was my answer. I told him that I was not sure. I went on to say that He might come in his lifetime, but he might come in his children's lifetime. The point is that we must always be prepared whenever he may return. We need to have our "Spiritual business" in order. After I told him this he asked, "How do we do this, Dad?" I simply gave him the facts with no "mumbo jumbo." I said to him that we need to pray at least three times a day; we need to ask for Gods help every day; we must treat other people like we want to be treated; and we need to follow the Ten Commandments.

All of this is a little difficult for a child to do but it is a Spiritual road map for them. If they do this when they grow up, and if they teach their children, and their children teach their children then it will not matter when Jesus will come because they will always be ready. I have developed a habit of trying to "get ready" every day. Some days I feel as though I did not do everything as good as I should have. Or perhaps I had certain wrong thoughts; but in general I always get back on track. This "system" that I developed is easy and designed for a person to get back on track. What I have decided to do everyday is pray three times a day to help remind me on what life is all about and to help me stay on track.

At one point in my life, it finally hit me that we need food everyday (and usually three times a day). Since our body needs physical nourishment three times a day, it just makes sense that our Spirits need nourishment three times a day, as well. Without a doubt, I believe that our Spirit needs nourishment every day. Just as a person may eat once daily to many times daily, I believe we need

Spiritual nourishment at least three times daily. Bottom line, I am 100% certain that our life is much better with Spiritual nourishment than without it. Just as I would never want to go a day without food, I decided a long time ago not to go a day without Spiritual food. I choose to pray everyday and more specifically, three times daily.

How I pray is not difficult; it does not consist of merely asking for a lot of things. It is the prayer that Jesus left for his APOSTLES. At one point, one of Jesus' Apostles asked Jesus how to pray? He described the "model prayer". As I mentioned previously, it is found in the book of Matthew, Chapter 6, verses 9-13. It goes like this.

"Our Father who art in Heaven hallowed be thy name. Your Kingdom come your will be done on Earth as it is in Heaven. Give us this day our daily bread and forgive us our trespasses as we forgive those who trespass against us, and lead us not into temptation but deliver us from evil. For thine is the Kingdom and power and the glory forever. Amen."

It is as easy as this. It is easy to say but really hard to do at times. This Lord's Prayer should be our daily guide. Just as we eat everyday (and likely three times daily), so should we say the Lord's Prayer three times a day. This prayer talks about praising God in Heaven, and waiting for His Kingdom to totally reign on this Earth without any interference from the Devil. It talks about our day-to-day physical and Spiritual food. It talks about asking forgiveness for doing things that are against God's will. It mentions forgiving others for bad things they may have done to us. And it says we are to ask God to deliver us from evil (the Devil). This prayer was given to us for us to say every day. He loved us so much that he wanted us to have a tool to fight the Devil to keep him from harming us. He knew (and still knows) that if the Devil "gets under our skin" and controls our bodies and minds we have no possible chance of finding health, happiness, and contentment; it will be impossible to accomplish.

The other thing I think of daily is the Ten Commandments. It is important to follow these commandments because they are designed to comfort our Soul, keep us from getting in trouble, and most importantly, to keep our mind focused on right things, so we may prepare to be with God. The commandments are as follows:

First Commandment: We should have no other God except the One that has created the Heavens and the Earth. This means that we should pray to Him daily even though we cannot see Him or understand it all. By doing this, our mindset should be that we make sure that we do not put importance on any other person, place, or thing.

Second Commandment: We should not make any graven image to the Lord. This means that we should not make some kind of statue or object and begin praying to what we have made. He wants us to understand that God is not an object but an eternal Spirit.

Third Commandment: We should not use God's name in vain. This means that we should never use God's name with a bad feeling behind it, or use it in a way we know is bad.

Fourth Commandment: Remember the Sabbath day and keep it holy. This day was originally set aside by the Jewish people before Jesus came to associate it to the creation of everything by God. This Sabbath day was established to give man a physical rest and a Spiritual uplifting, as well as a time of weekly remembrance. It was to remind the Jewish people they were the chosen ones of God. This day was celebrated from Friday's sunset to Saturday's sunset. Also on this day, the Jewish people were not to engage in any work of any kind.

However, when Jesus came to Earth, this somewhat changed. Though it was still the holy day (from Friday sunset to Saturday sunset), Jesus now added that this day was a day of remembrance and rest; people didn't need to have a "complete shutdown" of activities. He preached that doing works of mercy, even on the Sabbath, was acceptable to God. After Jesus died on the cross and was resurrected on the third day (which was Sunday), the followers of Christ (now called Christians) then chose Sunday to now be the Sabbath Day. Now, Sunday was to be used as the day of rest, the day of remembering God's creation of Heaven and Earth. Most important of all, remembering that Jesus came to Earth to show us a new way into Heaven by being nailed to a wooden cross; and after three days, he defied death and arose on that Sunday morning, that symbolic first day of the week. Since that time, the Sabbath was on the first day of the week for all Christians.

Fifth Commandment: Honor your father and mother. This is simple in nature, and for many years it was a sacred commandment (like them all). However, in the past few decades there has been a violent abuse of this commandment. Without a doubt, for almost two thousand years there has been a devotion to all mothers and fathers by their children. In essence, parents have taken care of their children and children have cared for their parents. It has been like an unwritten contract upheld by mostly everyone.

In the past few decades there has been a general breakdown in this time-honored contract. While there are many wonderful parents out there taking care of their children, there are just as many out there not taking care of their children. Children often grow up alone. Though they might have parents around, they likely are not an integral part of the children's minds. Children often are raised by their grandparents. On the other hand, children these days are often in an environment that is mentally and physically abusive. These conditions are not normal and often children grow up not having the love, time, or attention that they need to grow up mentally happy and sound.

When this kind of bad family vibrations happens for long periods of time the child grows up disliking their parents and sometimes hating them. This forces the children (who eventually become adults) who do not honor their fathers and mothers to break a commandment without them even knowing it. It is next to impossible to love someone (even if it is your parent) if you were treated like dirt as a child. The way to go back to implementing the fifth commandment is to take care of our children again.

Sixth Commandment: We should not kill. This is the simplest to understand of the commandments. It means that you and I should not go out and kill another human. Just because we are mad at someone does not mean that we should kill him or her. I am by no means an expert on why certain people go out and kill like serial killers; however, I do know that these people are filled with the Devil's Spirit. I do not know how we could stop the Devil from possessing their hearts and minds. But I know that we should defend ourselves from them. No human has the right to take our life and we should do whatever necessary to defend ourselves. God certainly doesn't want us killed, but the Devil does. The Devil's mindset is that the more that can be killed the better. As Christians, we may want to do well, but in the process we let other people trample all over us. Our good Lord does not want us to be trampled, that is why He gave us a mind to try to prevent someone trying to kill us.

Seventh Commandment: We should not commit adultery. This means that if we are married we should not "mouse around" with someone else. When people get married, they sign a contract with God and man; and they are obligated to stay committed to each other. However, the Devil loves to be the destroyer. He looks for every opportunity to get into a couple's relationship and somehow destroy it. Quite often he gets away with it and marriage falls apart. This situation puts the couple (and their children) through hard times. I know that sometimes the grass may seem a little greener on the other side; and maybe sometimes it is.

I am reminded of my lawn at home. For a while there it was always looking yellow and brown, no matter how much I watered it. One of my neighbors on the other hand had a lawn that looked great. One summer, I began to observe him and what he was doing differently than me. This gentleman was not only watering it but was systematically adding fertilizer and weed control to it throughout the season. We also started to do this and sure enough the weeds that were taking over the yard were leaving while the grass was getting greener.

A relationship is also like this. We need to add a little fertilizer to our relationship. Treating our spouse like we would like to be treated, taking care of each other and praying together. All couples should do this. We also need to add a little "weed killer" to our relationship. We need to kill any habit that we may have that is destructive to our marriage. Destructive habits in a relationship can be many. Just to name a few: drinking alcohol in excess, flirting with someone other than your spouse, doing things that you know bother the heck out of your spouse, and letting yourself get sloppy physically and mentally. If you can eliminate some of these habits you will not be put into a situation that you commit adultery.

Eighth Commandment: We should not steal. This simply means that if something is not yours do not take it. It is very tempting to take something that is not yours if you really need it, but it should not be done. There are people whom, for whatever reason, have developed a condition in their mind that they have to steal. This is called kleptomania. This compulsion is present whether a need for the money or goods exists or not. There is something about our human nature that, once in awhile, we feel like taking something (that isn't ours) when no one is around. For example, if we were walking down the street and found a twenty-dollar bill, our first reaction might be to say, "Oh, this is my lucky day!" After saying this, we might just look both ways and then shove it in our pocket. Even though we might not need the money at the time, our first reaction is just to take it.

Another situation I always think about takes place in a grocery store I often frequent. In this store they have a self-serve bakery section. Since I like sweet rolls, I often visit this place. At this bakery you choose which donuts you want and place them in a paper bag and go to the cash register. At the cash register the person there simply asks how many donuts you have; you tell her and she rings them up. Over the many times I've gone there, I've wondered if people took more donuts than they told the person at the cash register machine. Since the person at the cash register never checks to see if you are telling the truth, it is certainly possible. I always thought it would be extremely easy to lie to the person in charge; for example if you took three rolls, you could easily say you were only purchasing only two.

After a few years of going there and following this honor system, I noticed a change one day. The change was not in the rolls or the way they asked you how many rolls that you had; the change was in the kind of bags they used. The paper bags had been changed by the store for clear plastic bags. This was no big deal and nothing major had changed in the store the cash register attendant could merely see through the bag to see how many donuts a person chose to purchase. Seeing this change, I asked the person at the register why they had changed from paper bags to plastic. I knew what the answer might be but I wanted to see what she had to say. She went on to say that they had an unbelievable number of donuts that were unpaid for. For people to do this there must be an obvious problem with our human nature.

Forever in Your Debt

I personally believe that most everyone has been guilty of taking something that is not theirs. It could be a big item, money, or even something as small as a pencil. Other people have a mental condition which overtakes their better judgment and they steal. As mentioned previously, this condition is call kleptomania. At the store I was telling about earlier, I knew someone who works there that is an undercover security guard. His job is to catch people that are stealing. At one point, I had asked him if people often steal at their store? He said that the problem is so big that they have two full time people working to keep an eye on things. He went on to say that the people who steal are not only people that need things. He said that the people who steal come from all walks of life. They can be unemployed, have their own business, and be rich or poor. They have caught first time offenders and repeat offenders. He said that he was able to catch many people, but that a great many had not been caught.

I reason that a majority of people would not take anything in this fashion. I believe that the people who do so are good people with a problem. Even good people can have a problem with something like this. The good Lord knows that we have weaknesses; He wanted us to have this commandment of "Thou shalt not steal" to help His people stay on track. Over the years, the Devil somehow has put that bad seed (or trait) in us of stealing, and he wants it to continuously grow. The more the seeds of wrongdoing grow the more satisfied he is. He sees his mission in us like a beautiful garden that he wants to overtake with weeds. The Devil wants us to steal and not feel bad about it. God loves us and wants us to have the commandment of not stealing; this way, we will mentally have it as a tool to fight back. It is never too late to ask God for forgiveness in a silent prayer. Even if we get off track we can get back on. Bottom line, we should remember that if we really need something, instead of stealing we can borrow from a friend instead of stealing.

Ninth Commandment: We should not accuse someone of doing something if they did not do it. One of my favorite stories about this topic is a little silly, yet cute. I have three children (two boys and one girl). When my oldest son was nine years old, he had a wallet, which he liked a lot. In this wallet he keeps money that he has saved up. One day he ran to me with excitement and anger; he informed me that his wallet was missing and he knew who took it. So I asked him who it was. With 100% certainty, he knew it was his four year old brother. He then went on to tell me that he wanted to "pulverize him".

Forever in Your Debt

To calm him down before he "pulverized" his little brother, I brought it to his attention that perhaps his little brother had not taken it. My oldest son did not want to hear what I was saying. He knew that his young brother was guilty as charged and nothing was going to change his mind. He went on and on to say that his wallet was very important to him and his little brother was "going to pay for it." I kept trying to tell him to think about where he had it last and maybe, just maybe, he misplaced it. He didn't want to hear about it; the only thing that calmed him down was to tell him that I would help him look for it.

We looked and looked all over the house. After looking for the longest time, I caught a glimpse of it. It was in a long handled fishing net about six feet off the ground. This was a new fishing net in my oldest son's room that we had not used yet. I'm sure that my four your old could not have put it up there; it was simply too high off the ground. This was where my nine year old son would place things that he wanted to keep away from his little brother.

In the meantime, my oldest son was still looking for the wallet. Even though now I knew where his wallet was, I still called out to him and asked if he had found the wallet. He replied with a disappointed and angry voice, " No, I have not!" I proceeded to ask him again if he was sure that his little brother had taken it. He said, "Yes." I asked him if he was certain enough of this to place a bet on it. He agreed. We agreed that if he was right he could take something from his younger brother. But if he was wrong, he would have to give his younger brother a big hug, an apology, and something that belonged to him. My oldest son, so sure of his mindset, agreed to the bet.

Throughout all of this high stakes betting, I never let on that I knew where the wallet was. All along, my four year old son was saying that he didn't take the wallet. Of course, this did not mean anything to my oldest son, because he was sure that his little brother was guilty. As I was trying to keep a straight face throughout all of this I told my oldest son to go back to his room with me and look again. He assured me that he checked his room inside and out. I convinced him to check once again together. After searching again, I casually mentioned to him that maybe he could have placed his wallet in the net. He immediately jumped up and knew it was in the net without even looking! It hit him that he had not checked in the most obvious spot he used to keep things out of his little brother's hands…the fishing net! I made him look in there just to make sure he saw it, and once again he was happy. After a couple of minutes I reminded him of the deal we had made. It was unbearable to him to "pay up"; he had to give a hug, apologize, as well as give a little something to his little brother. But, in the end, he was paid in full!

It is easy for all of us to accuse people of doing something wrong. It is easy for us to talk about others; it is easy to gossip and spread rumors. But all of this behavior is destructive for mankind. God believed it was so important, that he left this commandment for us to follow. The Devil wants us to talk about each other in a destructive way. He wants us to spread false rumors. He wants us to be mad at everyone. Our good Lord does not want us to hate each other; He does not want us to spread rumors, and he does not want us to accuse others unless we are 100% sure. It is sometimes next to impossible to treat certain people nicely but He wants us to try.

Tenth Commandment: Do not be jealous of each other; do not desire what others have. In the times we live in (and every other period of time before us) people have always been jealous of other people. There is no question in my mind that, in most of our lives, we all have been a little jealous from time to time. This usually happens when one of our friends or relatives has something that we want or need. It could be a better car, a better house, a better job, or even a better spouse! It sure is easy to be jealous of someone if you do not have much. In my experience the people that are usually the most jealous are the ones that already have nice things but seem to want more. I do not believe there is anything wrong with wanting nice things, but there is a problem of wanting more and more. There is a deep-seated problem in continuing to want; it leads to jealousy. This behavior will eventually overtake you, if you let it. If you have many riches and flaunt them to make others jealous, then you are in the same category as the jealous ones!

If a person has a lot of stuff they should never show it off to someone who has less. Especially if a person has a lot less. Showing off things hurts people and can create negative feelings. I would like to share another story with you. It is a story of a businessman that I once knew. He always wanted to show off the things that he had. At one point in his life he bought a large expensive, shiny watch. It was a kind of watch that was meant to be seen. One day this gentleman was at a Mall and had to use the restroom. He headed to the restroom with his expensive suit, and while in the restroom he was hit on the head from behind. When he came to (after someone had found him) he quickly realized that his expensive watch was stolen. It was a tragic situation in that the businessman not only lost his watch but also got a concussion, and lost some of his health. He was never the same after that. The man who took the watch was eventually caught and was prosecuted. This was a clear situation that both men lost. The attacker wanted that watch so badly that he would do anything to get it. The businessman wanted to show off his watch so much that he ended up paying a heavy price for his pride.

All of this happened over a watch. It was not the watch's fault but an inherent weakness in us. The Devil has tainted us with that trait somewhere along in our development. Of course, our good Lord saw this and knew it was a destructive thing for mankind; so he gave us a tool that we could use to fight the Devil. If you are a person that does not have a lot of things, don't worry about it. God loves you just as much as a billionaire. If you are a person who has a lot things, don't worry about losing them; God loves you the same. If you do not have the things you want or need, just slowly work for them, and don't be jealous of the person who has these things already.

If you are the one with lots of things, don't "rub it in" or flaunt your goods to anyone, especially if that person does not have much. Never lose sight of the fact that we are only here on this Earth for a short while and then we have to cross the bridge to the other World. The Devil judges you on how miserable and bad you can be; he wants to take you with him to the land of eternal misery. On the other hand, God judges you and me on our moral character and kindness; He wants us to be with Him for eternity when we cross that bridge. The Devil will always want you to fail in this quest, but our great Lord wants us to forever succeed.

Chapter Ten

FOREVER IN YOUR DEBT

I hope that you have enjoyed this book. Most important though, I sure hope that I was able to share with you some knowledge that I have learned along the way that might make your life a little better and smoother. Without a doubt, this life can be very difficult if we do not have some kind of plan to help us get through it. We seem to just allow everybody and their brother to show us what is right or wrong in our lives. We allow people in Hollywood to make movies and television shows that determine what we should look like, be like, and feel like. We need to go back to good, old-fashioned common sense thinking. We need to try to read and follow the roadmap that God has laid out for us. I know we live in a new and modern time, but certain values are timeless, and never get old.

First of all, we need to take care of ourselves by doing good things that we know are good for us and avoid doing things that are destructive. Destructive things that are not good for us are over eating, over drinking, over working, flirting around with someone besides your spouse or even listening to people that you know are not looking out for your best interests.

Second, it is paramount to treat your spouse with respect and dignity. This can be difficult at times because many people have never been treated with love and respect, so they do not know how to give it. If you are the one trying to be nice, give love and respect. Do not be surprised if the person that you are trying to give this to does not know how to handle it. It might be a shock for them because they may have never received this kind of treatment! Whatever the case, treating your spouse well is a timeless value and needs to be done.

Third, if you have children, treat them how you would like to have been treated when you were a child. If you do not have children, treat all children that you come across this way. There is too much physical and mental abuse in our World. Often, we get mad at something and lash out at someone else. If life is getting you down, you are not alone. Instead of lashing out at your children, go for a long walk or jog. Maybe you could get a punching bag and punch on that. Though it sounds simple, this really works. You will feel better for letting out your frustrations on the bag instead of your children! Remember that you would not want to be physically or mentally abused when you were a child. When abusing a child, you are really

Forever in Your Debt

abusing yourself because half of your child's genes come from you.

Fourth, treat other people with respect. Whether they are old, young, black, yellow, green, they all deserve respect. When you see someone in the street, give him or her a good old-fashioned smile. It will make you feel better and will make them feel better. There is a Spiritual war going on at all times. On one side God is leading the charge of good, positive, pure thinking people. On the other side, there is the Devil leading the charge of bad, negative, "gutter thinking people". Just like in a physical war when one side is trying to physically kill the other side, a Spiritual war is the same. God wants every single person on this Earth to be on His side and be happy, healthy, and harmonious. The Devil wants everyone on this Earth to take his side and be unhappy, unhealthy, and miserable.

This war just did not begin recently. It has been going on since shortly after God placed Adam and Eve here on this Earth. The Devil got to Eve, and this war has been raging ever since. This war is a silent war. This is a war of the two forces (good and evil) and is constantly being fueled by the Devil. God does not want this Spiritual war to exist. He wants a permanent resolution to take place. He wants everything in this World to be peaceful. The Devil also wants a permanent resolution to happen.

However, he wants total chaos in our lives. He wants to be the spoiler in everything that we do. Somehow and some way, he spoiled the perfect relationship that God had with Adam and Eve. He also wants to spoil the relationship you and I have with God. The more people he gets on his side of this Spiritual warfare the more destruction he can cause. If this happens, it means more destruction on this Planet, which will result in more sorrow. This will result in him having more control over our lives.

When this happens we will be totally enslaved to him. The more enslaved we are to him the less happy we will be. The more enslaved we are to him the less healthy we will be. The more enslaved we are to him the less content we will be. If this continues, then these feelings and traits will be passed on down to our children and their children; in a few generations we will be at his total mercy, forever in bondage. The only hope of breaking the chains of this destructive pattern is through the awesome power of the Creator of the Heaven and Earth, God Himself. God wants so badly for us to be free from the claws of the Devil that He has armed us with the dual weapons of a heart and mind. With these weapons (and a reliance upon the Eternal Spirit), we can overcome the Evil One. He gave us a heart and mind to be able to read, hear and understand the Ten Commandments and the other writings of the Bible. God sent his only Son to Earth, which took the form of a man; He was filled with God's Spirit to show the World, two thousand years ago, (as well as today) that the Devil can be overcome...and eventually destroyed.

The Devil thought he had killed God's Son a couple of thousand years ago. He thought that he could give people of that age (as well as future generations) misery forever but he was not smart and powerful. Jesus, operating in complete obedience to God's will, spoiled the Devil's plan. God, through His own will, allowed his only Son that He sent to planet Earth to be tortured by the Devil. The Devil put Him through much misery before his death, and eventually watched Him suffer by being nailed to a wooden cross. It was not God's Mission to watch His Son suffer and die; it was God's Mission to prove to the physical World that the Devil can be beaten. God allowed His Son to die on that cross. Jesus was in the World of the dead for three somber days. After those three days our great and powerful Lord set his Son free and brought him back to life. All of this was done for everyone in the World to see forever that the Devil can be fought and defeated.

However, we must do our part in the war against the Devil. We need to treat ourselves well. We need to treat our spouses with love and respect.

We need to treat our children with love and not neglect them. We need to treat people around us with kindness whether they are neighbors, friends, or relatives. It is also very important to be conscious of something else. We must be keen and smart to not allow the Devil's people to rob us of our quest for happiness, our quest for being healthy, or our quest for being content. Therefore, if a person is trying to make our life miserable we must fight back. We should be like a Christian Warrior. A Christian Warrior is someone who is conscious and alert to the situation and circumstances around him. They recognize that there is a problem and they do something about it.

The first thing they always do is ask God in a silent prayer what to do. It can be as simple as praying, "Lord, I am in a situation that I do not like, please guide me to make the right decision."

Second, a Christian Warrior in this stressful situation must remember to pick up the Bible and read it…at any place in the scriptures. Look upon it as if someone attacked you. You need to pick up something like a stick, bat, or pole (any object, really) to fight back. A Christian Warrior uses God's word to fight in battle. This is why the Apostle Paul in the New Testament Book of Ephesians, Chapter 6 and verse 17, says,

"And take the ...sword of the Spirit which is the Word of God."

Third, do not be anxious on what to do next. You will be guided in your next move without even realizing it. In reading the Bible for help do not sit there day in and day out reading it. God has given those pages as a tool to use, not for us to be a slave to them. Those pages are for us to get comfort, joy, and direction. By no means does the Devil want you to get any comfort, joy, and find direction.

Don't you think it is worthwhile to consciously think about this and try to fight the Devil? Don't you think it is worthwhile to fight not only for ourselves but also for our children? I know it is an awesome feat to try and make this World a place where God is the only ruler. God needs us to help Him. God is giving us the cup full of the water of health, the water of happiness and the water of contentment. The only thing we need to do is take the cup and drink it. We will then have a chance at living a life with more happiness. We will then have a chance at living a life that is healthier. We will then have a chance at a life that is filled with more contentment. Purpose in your heart to be forever in God's debt and you will have all these blessings. As Jesus said in Matthew, Chapter 6, verse 33,

Dr. Nick Dreliozis

"Seek first the Kingdom of God and His righteousness, and all these things shall be added unto you."

The End